G000245695

CONCERNING AGNES

Thomas Hardy's 'Good Little Pupil'

Desmond Hawkins

ALAN
SUTTON
1982

Alan Sutton Publishing Limited
17a Brunswick Road
Gloucester

First published 1982

Copyright © 1982 Desmond Hawkins

All rights reserved. No part of this publication may be reproduced, stored in a retrieval system, or transmitted, in any form or by any means, electronic, mechanical photocopying, recording or otherwise, without the prior permission of the publishers and copyright holder.

British Library Cataloguing in Publication Data

Hawkins, Desmond
Concerning Agnes: Thomas Hardy's 'good little pupil'
1. Grove, Agnes Geraldine, *Lady*
I. Title
941.081'092'4 DA565.G/

ISBN 0-904387-97-6

Typesetting and origination by
Alan Sutton Publishing Limited.
Photoset Janson 10/12
Printed in Great Britain
by Page Bros (Norwich) Limited

List of Illustrations

Dedicated to Richard Little Purdy
in recognition of the debt owed to him by all students
of Thomas Hardy's writings; and with my added gratitude
for his foresight and care in preserving Agnes Grove's
personal papers concerning Hardy.

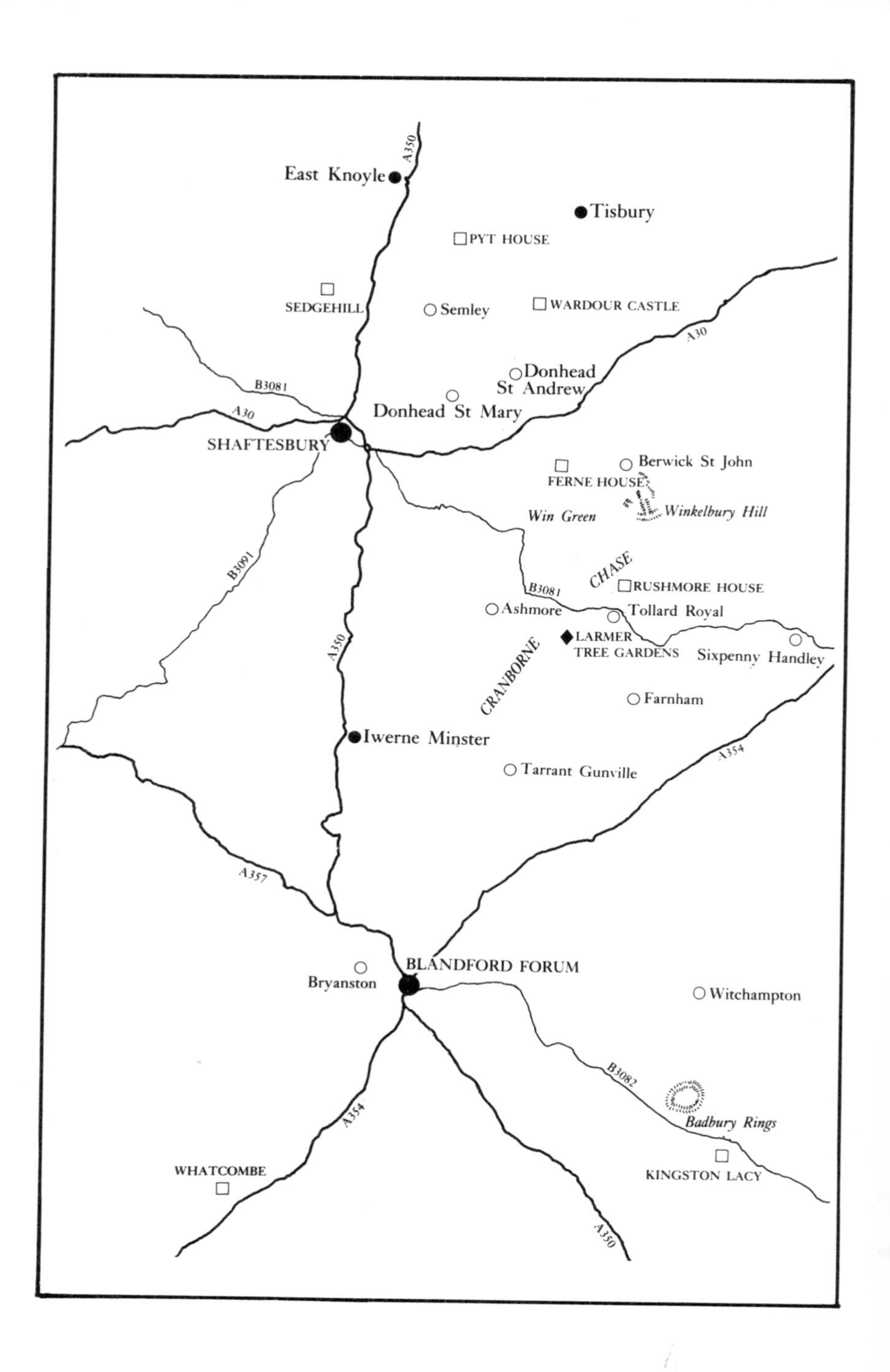

A350
East Knoyle
Tisbury
PYT HOUSE
SEDGEHILL
Semley
WARDOUR CASTLE
A30
Donhead
St Andrew
Donhead St Mary
B3081
A30
SHAFTESBURY
Berwick St John
FERNE HOUSE
Win Green
Winkelbury Hill
B3091
CHASE
RUSHMORE HOUSE
B3081
Ashmore
Tollard Royal
LARMER
TREE GARDENS
Sixpenny Handley
A350
CRANBORNE
Farnham
Iwerne Minster
A354
Tarrant Gunville
A357
BLANDFORD FORUM
Bryanston
Witchampton
B3082
Badbury Rings
A354
WHATCOMBE
KINGSTON LACY
A350

Introduction

In the course of some research preparatory to the publication in 1976 of *Hardy: novelist and poet* I became interested in the identity of the subject of one of Hardy's poems. Its title, 'Concerning Agnes', was not very revealing but a reference in it to 'the Larmer avenue' whetted my curiosity. 'Larmer' is an unusual word and I had for some years been familiar with the Larmer Tree Gardens, created by the eminent archaeologist General Augustus Pitt-Rivers at Tollard Royal in Wiltshire. It was not difficult to discover that 'Agnes' was one of the General's daughters, that she had been the wife of Sir Walter Grove, and that some of her letters to Thomas Hardy were preserved in the Dorset County Museum.

To these simple facts there clung the legend of a woman of keen wit and outstanding beauty, a child of the Whig aristocracy whose cousins included Bertrand Russell. As I talked to those who had known her I felt I must make an effort to recapture something of the living presence that had inspired Hardy's poem.

It was my good fortune to enjoy the most generous support from descendants of the two families, Pitt-Rivers and Grove. Michael Pitt-Rivers, the present owner of the Larmer Tree Gardens, and Anthony Pitt-Rivers allowed me to inspect family papers and photos in their possession. On the Grove side I must anticipate my narrative by mentioning Katherine, Kate or 'Kat' Grove, as she was variously called. When her brother Walter married Agnes the two women formed a close friendship which their children continued. To one of Kate's daughters, the late Vivien Pleydell-Railstone of Whatcombe, I am deeply indebted for access to a voluminous assortment of archival documents, letters, photo albums and miscellaneous papers deposited at Whatcombe by Agnes's children and other members of the Grove family. Since the death of Mrs. Pleydell-Railstone her daughter, Patricia Chichester, has kindly made me feel no less welcome at Whatcombe. A further source of great assistance has been the Grove family solicitors, in the person of Michael Carey, for whose patience and courteous forbearance over several years I am most grateful. Many of the papers entrusted to me to study have since been deposited in the Wiltshire Record Office at Trowbridge. For the opportunity to examine the Pitt-Rivers papers in the S. Wilts Museum at Salisbury, and the Hardy Collection in the Dorset County Museum, I am obliged to the respective curators, Peter Saunders and Roger Peers.

In addition to this substantial body of unpublished source material I must emphasise my indebtedness to Professor R.L. Purdy, the present owner of Hardy's letters to Agnes, for allowing me to study and publish some extracts from them before their inclusion in full in the magnificent volumes of Hardy's entire correspondence which he and Michael Millgate are now completing for the Clarendon Press: I hope my biography of Agnes will serve as an extended footnote to that correspondence. My first acount of Hardy's relationship with Agnes appeared in *Encounter* in February 1977, for which I offer the customary acknowledgement to the editors.

I also wish to record my gratitude to Robert Gittings for drawing my attention to the published recollections of Jacques-Emile Blanche; to Pauline Spender for unearthing the exchange of lettres between Agnes and George Bernard Shaw; to the late Ronald Farquharson and Daphne Arnold-Foster for valuable reminiscences; and to my daughter, Teresa, for deciphering and transcribing the hurried and sometimes barely legible scrawl in which Agnes's diary-entries were written.

For permission to reprint the letter by George Bernard Shaw I am grateful to the Society of Authors; and to A.D. Peters Ltd. for two letters by Hilaire Belloc. For brief extracts of copyright material I must thank George Allen and Unwin, the publishers of Bertrand Russell's autobiography; and A.D. Peters Ltd. for part of a letter from the Stanley family correspondence edited by Nancy Mitford in *The Stanleys of Alderley* (Hamish Hamilton). Acknowledgements for photos are included with a select bibliography at the end of the book (page 142).

Thomas Hardy's 'Good Little Pupil'

As with my previous book, *Cranborne Chase*, Ann Bellchambers has pleased my publishers by producing a final typescript which, for elegance and clarity, surpasses any tune I could get out of a typewriter.

Desmond Hawkins
Blandford 1981

Chapter One

In December 1926 Thomas Hardy received the news that one more of his old friends had died. Florence Hardy dutifully wrote a note of condolence on their behalf, and the son of the deceased woman sent to Max Gate a touching reply which Florence preserved. 'She was the centre of our world and without her we seem utterly lost.' Presumably Florence showed the letter to Hardy, and the old man – he was then eighty-six – pondered on the event. Soon afterwards he took up his pen and headed a sheet of paper with the two words 'Concerning Agnes'. What followed was the tender and moving elegy that opens with the lines –

> I am stopped from hoping what I have hoped before –
>   Yes, many a time! –
> To dance with that fair woman yet once more
>   As in the prime
> Of August, when the wide-faced moon looked through
> The boughs at the faery lamps of the Larmer Avenue.

The poem appeared two years later in *Winter Words*, a few months after Hardy himself had died. The identity of Agnes was not revealed but – as in other poems about the 'fair women' who stirred his romantic impulse – the poet incorporated an unmistakable clue. The only time Hardy danced under 'the faery lamps of the Larmer Avenue' was in September 1895 when he and his first wife, Emma, spent a few days at Rushmore as the guests of General Pitt-Rivers. The General had inherited the Rivers estates in 1880, an unexpected stroke of fortune which obliged him to change his name from Lane

Fox to Pitt-Rivers and which gave him the opportunity to undertake the pioneer work in archaeology on which his fame rests. He had other outlets, however, for his wealth and imaginative energy, and one of them was the Pleasure Gardens that he created at an ancient local landmark, the Larmer Tree. Here he assembled buildings from the Indian Exhibition at Earl's Court, an openair theatre and other buildings and follies of his own design in the *ferme ornée* tradition, grouped in a spacious garden. It was a popular attraction in the nineties, particularly for visitors to the rapidly growing resort of Bournemouth, less than twenty miles away.

The invitation to the Hardys to visit Rushmore in September was clearly timed to synchronise with the great annual event at the Larmer Tree Gardens – a day devoted to sports, horse racing, a concert and general festivities which culminated in dancing on the lawns by the light of thousands of Vauxhall lamps. Hardy must have been pleased and impressed by the occasion for he preserved a newspaper cutting describing the scene. Twenty years later, when he was preparing his autobiography, he quoted extensively from this account in what he called 'the local paper'; it was in fact the *Dorset County Chronicle* and its description included a reference to some country dances 'started by the house-party and led off by the beautiful Mrs. Grove, the daughter of General Pitt-Rivers'.

To the words of the local journalist Hardy added his own comments in *The Life of Thomas Hardy*, emphasising that 'It was he who started the country dances, his partner being the above-mentioned Mrs. (afterwards Lady) Grove'. In a later reference Hardy refers to her similarly as 'the beautiful Mrs., afterwards Lady, Grove'. She was the Agnes whose death thirty years later inspired in him the wish to have over again

> That old romance,
> And sit apart in the shade as we sat then
> After the dance
> The while I held her hand.

Just what was she like, this beautiful daughter of the General who made such an instant impression on the poet? She certainly had a striking pedigree, compounded of Pitts and Stanleys. To Hardy she must have seemed the embodiment of the great dynasties that ruled much of Victorian England. In his native village, Stinsford, a familiar sight in the church was the bust of George Pitt whose descendants held the lordship of Cranborne Chase and the title of Baron Rivers. It was through his Pitt grandmother that Agnes's father came into his great inheritance.

With just so much to go on it is easy enough to imagine an aristocratic young woman whose beauty must have been displayed at some time in an Academy portrait; and so indeed it was. But to give a semblance of animation to the pale shadows of the past one needs more such parings of the living spirit – letters, diaries, photos, reminiscences – which may by chance survive. Fortunately Agnes and her family tended to hoard things, or at least to lack the will to discard them. Her diaries and engagement books for most of her adult life have been preserved: so have the love letters that Walter Grove sent her, the wrangling correspondence of parents and lawyers over her marriage settlement, her own letters to her husband and her children, and the letters she received from Thomas Hardy and other eminent authors. To all these the published letters of her mother's family, the Stanleys of Alderley, add a rich background.

What emerges is not an undiscovered genius or an unexpected saint but a woman, simply, whose story is worth telling. To know her is to have a personal insight into that society of wealth and privilege which had its last fling in Edwardian England and disintegrated in the Great War of 1914. She had all her human share of folly and selfishness, but at least they were offset by her vitality and her sense of style. She cared deeply about many things and she fought in her own way for her aspirations and her ideals.

The earliest expression of her individuality dates from 1 January 1879 when she was a schoolgirl of fifteen, or more precisely – as she would have wished – fifteen and a half. On that first day of the new year she signed herself 'Agnes Lane Fox' on the flyleaf of her diary before making her first and not very inspired entry –

> Saw new year in at the Howards. Having supper – great fun.
> Howards came to luncheon – had fun.

The Howards are not difficult to identify. Agnes's maternal aunt, Rosalind Stanley, had married George Howard, Earl of Carlisle, in 1864. Their two eldest children, Mary and Charles, were contemporaries, cousins and childhood companions of Agnes. During the school holidays of January 1879 there were frequent visitings exchanged between the young Howards and Foxes, and they were not always unalloyed fun. On 11 January Agnes noted that, during an afternoon visit to the Howards, she 'got into rather a row for quarrelling'. This suggests she was already showing the hot imperious temper and zest for family strife which were so characteristic of the Stanleys and were later exemplified in full measure by herself.

The rest of the holiday was occupied with German lessons and visits to the theatre. Her hope of going to *Hamlet* was dashed because all the seats were booked, but she sat in a ducal box at Drury Lane to see *Cinderella* and she marvelled at the magic of 'Maskelyne & Cooke's'. On 20 January life became real and earnest again: Aunt Maude Stanley bought her a bible, took her to the station and saw her off to the new term at Oxford High School.

It was a hard winter, that year. Most days there was skating and 16 February brought a snowstorm. Agnes suffered from chilblains – that scourge of children in unheated boarding schools. To combat the cold she slept in her clothes. By half-term an illness halted her diary entries for several weeks and when she returned to it, on 31 March, it was to inscribe the large initials 'X.T' – which perhaps indicate the end of the school term.

Part of the Easter holiday she spent at Guildford. Her diary is uneventful and sometimes blank during this period, but an entry for 16 April has an historical interest. It reads 'played l.t.' – an early reference to lawn tennis, which was the new craze in English society. In this same year, 1879, Richard Jefferies, in 'Hodge and his Masters', referred to people 'playing tennis in appropriate costume'. Two years later, in 'A Laodicean', Thomas Hardy described 'some young people who were so madly devoted to lawn-tennis that they set about it like day-labourers at the moment of their arrival'. The game, which was not invented until the 1870s, seems to have established itself very quickly in the southern counties among Agnes's contemporaries.

Back at school she closed her diary until 25 July, her sixteenth birthday, when she wrote 'Came back home, Mama and Lionel met me at Paddington. Had some strawberries directly I got home.' The note of quiet exultation will not be lost on anyone who recalls a similar start to the summer holidays.

Lionel was one of Agnes's six brothers, only three years her senior and probably the one to whom she felt closest. The three eldest sons – Alex, St. George and Willy – were already men in their early twenties and therefore somewhat remote from a schoolgirl. The two youngest – Douglas and Arthur – were respectively only one year and three years younger than Agnes but she seems to have had little intimacy with them. Much stronger were her relationships with her two sisters. Ursula was four years older than Agnes, Alice only eighteen months older, and it is evident that the three sisters had in common a single-minded intention to find suitable husbands and set up their own establishments as quickly as possible. Ursula, as the eldest girl, was the first to escape from the somewhat tyrannical atmosphere of family life, in which Alice and Agnes formed a pact of mutual support against the frustrations imposed by their parents.

In the summer of 1879 relief for Ursula was already in sight. One of the tennis parties noted by Agnes was at Thorpe, near Egham, where she, Ursula, Lionel and their mother were visiting. Their tennis partners were young Scotts and Blacketts, the Scotts being kinsfolk: before her marriage General Scott's wife was Hon. Harriett Alethea Stanley, sister of the second Lord Stanley and therefore Ursula's great-aunt. Her son, Willy Scott, was sad when the visit came to an end. Agnes recalled that he 'had got two lovely bunches of flowers, one for me, one for Urs'. It was tactful to treat both sisters the same: a year later he married Ursula.

Looking at the names in Agnes's diary one realises how much her social world consisted of kinsfolk. Julia Dillon, Frank Russell and Lady Conyers – to instance three – were no chance acquaintances. Agnes's maternal grandmother was a Dillon. Frank Russell, two years younger than Agnes, was the elder son of Agnes's aunt Kate. He and his younger brother, Bertrand Russell, were therefore Agnes's cousins. Lady Conyers was the wife of Sackville George Lane Fox, who became the twelfth Baron Conyers. Their daughter, Marcia, was one of Agnes's closer friends.

And of course there were always aunts to be visited. After the tennis parties in Surrey Agnes went off 'by express' to Brighton for a fortnight where she lunched with aunt Fabia and went to see aunt Sara at Regency Square. Aunt Fabia was an interesting character, a Spanish lady whose marriage to uncle Henry, the third Lord Stanley, was clouded by a suspicion that Fabia had a previous husband still living somewhere. Loyal to her brother Mrs. Pitt-Rivers had been among the first to welcome his Spanish bride.

From Brighton Agnes, accompanied doubtless by Mama, moved on to Bognor at the start of September, staying at 1 Alex Terrace, bathing and playing tennis, visiting Lady Cecilia Bingham and enjoying the last days of relative freedom before the inevitable return to Oxford and the daily trivialities of a schoolgirl's life which she now scorned to record in her diary. The little book contains only one further entry –

19 December: 'Left Oxford for good.'

Chapter Two

The events of 1880, so far as they concerned Agnes, remain largely unchronicled. No longer a schoolgirl she probably followed particular lines of study appropriate to her circumstances. Living with her family at Earl's Court she could have continued the German lessons of the previous year and have begun the instruction in art to which she later referred. If she kept a diary it has not survived. Perhaps there was nothing much to write about at first, apart from Ursula's marriage to Willy Scott.

June brought a transformation, however; and in one sense a literal one, for Agnes Geraldine Lane Fox was transformed by royal licence into Agnes Geraldine Fox-Pitt. With the change of name went a change in the family fortunes which must initially have been difficult to grasp in its full significance. By the death without issue of Horace Pitt-Rivers, the sixth Lord Rivers, the entire Rivers estate passed to Agnes's father, with the condition that he assume the name of Pitt-Rivers. The London Gazette of 4 June gave effect to the new names. The General was authorised to adopt the new surname and to bear the arms of Pitt heraldically, and his children to add the surname of Pitt after that of Fox.

As a senior officer the General had settled into a style of living that could be described as comfortable rather than affluent. With nine children to support he certainly had no margin for extravagance. His marriage in 1853 to Alice Stanley, eldest daughter of Lord Stanley of Alderley, had not greatly pleased the Stanleys who had a talent for prosperous dynastic alliances at the altar: they were not impressed by a Guards officer who had all the strategic disadvantages of being the younger son of a younger son. But then who could foresee that Death would so assiduously remove the prior claimants?

By his interitance General Pitt-Rivers became probably the largest owner of land in Dorset, with further territory in neighbouring Wiltshire. Rushmore Lodge in the parish of Berwick St. John was his principal seat, with King John's House at Tollard Royal and the lovely manor house at Hinton St. Mary as additional residences. This little kingdom had been held by the Pitts since 1714. The Rivers barony was created for George Pitt, the fourth of that name in successive generations, in 1776. The male line had already failed once, in 1828, when the second baron was succeeded by his sister's son, William Horace Beckford, who thereupon adopted the name of Pitt-Rivers rather than his uncle's simple 'Pitt' – perhaps as a precaution in case the Rivers title did not come automatically to him with his inheritance of the estate. In his case the fear was groundless whereas the General spent twenty years in the reasonable expectation – never fulfilled – that the Rivers title would be similarly revived for him. In spite of his distinguished military career, his growing fame in scientific circles as an archaeologist and his public-spirited service as the first Inspector of Ancient Monuments General Pitt-Rivers died a commoner.

Rushmore Lodge, which is now a school, has a long history. It stands within what were known as the Lesser Bounds of Cranborne Chase, when the deer preserves of the Chase were divided into Walks – each Walk having its Ranger's or Keeper's Lodge. There is an interesting reference to Rushmore in Henry VIII's reign, when money was provided 'for repairs made upon the Lodge of Rushmore within the Chase of Cranborne by the Ranger there this year with the consent of the Queen's counsellors'. As Lord of the Chase King Henry made it a part of his wife's jointure, while she remained queen. What this meant is quietly symbolised by two shields-of-arms in the windows above the chancel arch of the church at nearby Tarrant Gunville. One displays the arms of Henry VIII impaling those of Katherine Parr, while in the other the King's arms impale those of Katherine Howard. Both Katherines enjoyed the use of Rushmore – for a time.

The modern history of Rushmore really begins in 1671 when James Cecil, the third earl of Salisbury, decided to sell the lordship of the Chase and thereby severed its link with Cranborne manor which he retained. In the next forty years the lordship passed through several hands before it came to George Pitt in 1714. As lord of the Chase Pitt now owned the exclusive right to preserve and hunt deer, and to impose the laws of vert and venison on other landowners throughout the territory within the bounds of the Chase: what he lacked was a local seat to take over the role traditionally filled by Cranborne. The answer was Rushmore, which provided the necessary offices for his steward and served as a hunting box for the family when they came to hunt.

In about 1760 the old building at Rushmore was replaced by something more to the taste of George Pitt IV, later to become the first Baron Rivers of Stratfieldsaye. In 1794 an Enclosure Act added 776 acres of pasture and woodland to the Rushmore estate, making it – in the words of Charles Bowles – 'a most desirable residence for any nobleman or gentleman who may be fond of retirement and rural sports.' When Stratfieldsaye was sold to the nation, to be presented to the Duke of Wellington after his final defeat of Napoleon, Rushmore had an added importance for the Pitts as their principal summer residence.

The arrival of the young Fox-Pitts with their parents in 1880 must have been an exciting and tonic event for the servants at Rushmore and the inhabitants of the surrounding villages, Tollard Royal, Sixpenny Handley, Berwick St. John, Ashmore and Tarrant Gunville. Rushmore needed an infusion of new blood and youthful vitality. The last Lord Rivers had been a childless man of 53 when he succeeded his young nephew. For thirteen years he served as a kind of caretaker in a role he had not anticipated since his elder brother, the fourth Baron, had thirteen children including four sons. The irruption of the Fox Pitts must have prompted some of the older inhabitants to recall that earlier family circle of children at Rushmore and the weird fate that overcame them. The tale of the gipsy's curse would have been told again, many times no doubt – the curse of the betrayed gipsy woman who prophesied the extinction of the Rivers dynasty.

You may believe or disbelieve in the efficacy of curses but it is a fact that Death was a frequent visitor to Rushmore in the 1850s. The eldest son and heir to the title was sixteen when he died. The next in line died at seventeen. His younger brother enjoyed only fourteen years of life. When news of this pervasive ill-health reached Lord Stanley the thought occurred to him that his daughter's marriage to Major Lane Fox might not prove to be so unrewarding after all. He decided to visit Rushmore in 1858, scenting the possibility that if the young Pitts continued to die at this rate the family connection with the Lane Foxes through their Pitt grandmother might – just conceivably – be to the advantage of his son-in-law. The account of the visit that Lord Stanley sent in a letter to his wife gives an interesting picture of Rushmore at that time.

> 'This is, I believe, the only place in England eighteen miles from a railway station. It takes as long to come from Salisbury as from London to Salisbury. The road is all over a down country and the house here is situated at the top of the highest hills on this high downy country, 800 feet they say above the sea. Immediately within sight of the house the country is bleak open downs, but below there is an immense extent of beautiful wild wood, the remains of old Cranborne Chase and rough ground with old thorns scattered on the open downs. The estate goes for 20 miles, with no neighbours.'

The purpose of the letter, however, was not to expatiate on the Rushmore landscape but to assess the health of its occupants. Coming to the point in a single sentence Lord Stanley concluded, 'I saw the eldest son carried out by a servant and put into a little carriage – he cannot walk at all and is not likely to live; they say the younger one is better than his brother, but I suspect not much'.

The older boy was indeed dead within a year. The younger one staved off the inevitable for a further eight years while in the meantime both his parents died and – as if a malign impatience intervened – one of his sisters on her honeymoon was struck by lightning and killed. They were not a lucky family.

By contrast fortune must have seemed to shine with unexampled brightness on the Fox-Pitts in that summer of 1880 when Agnes had her seventeenth birthday and began to explore the new world of Rushmore and the Chase villages. The park in which the mansion stood was suitably vast. Its north lodge gate opened on to a minor road which joined a section of the ancient ridgeway known as the Ox Drove before winding down the slopes of Winkelbury Hill to the village of Berwick St. John. The south lodge led to the turnpike road – now the B3081 – between Sixpenny Handley and Tollard Royal.

Although it lies just within the parish of Berwick St. John, Rushmore is much closer to the village of Tollard Royal. It was Tollard church that tended to be regarded as their parish church by the family at Rushmore, and it was in Tollard that General Pitt-Rivers created the Larmer Tree Gardens, where Agnes first met Thomas Hardy. That lay in the future, however. In 1880 it is more important to consider Agnes's discovery of the Ox Drove and Berwick St. John and what lay beyond.

Passing through the gates of the lodge at the northern end of the park – Bridmere Lodge – she would have come to one of the finest views the Chase can offer. The land rises here to a dramatic escarpment with Win Green as its highest point, 910 feet above sea level. From Win Green the ridgeway follows the edge of the escarpment along Monks Down to Winkelbury Hill, which juts out in a long steepsided promontory crowned with an Iron Age fort. Down below are Berwick St. John and the grounds of Ferne House. Beyond them the land sweeps up again in another spectacular climb to the summit of Whitesheet Hill and the old coachroad from Shaftesbury to Salisbury.

If we may imagine Agnes and her father standing here together, savouring the magnificent prospect, there is no doubt what would seize the General's attention. The tell-tale irregularities on the surface of Winkelbury must have stirred the archaeologist in him. Within a year he began his excavation here. But Agnes? She must have noticed the great mansion in the grounds at Ferne and perhaps have wondered if any of her own age and class lived there. Suitable companions were not conspicuously abundant in the vicinity. Tollard Royal contained only her father's tenants. Sixpenny Handley and Farnham similarly were part of the Rivers estate. Tarrant Gunville had what remained of the great palace at Eastbury that Sir John Vanbrugh built in the eighteenth century for Bubb Dodington; but it had been converted by Squire Farquharson to a humbler use as his hunting kennels.

All this made Ferne House more interesting potentially. It was the home of the Grove family who had lived there since Elizabethan times. The present owner was Sir Thomas Grove, a member of Parliament in the Liberal interest and a keen fox hunter who was described as 'a big man riding big horses – he made the fences easier for those that followed him.' As a landowner he was in the same league as Pitt-Rivers and their estates bordered each other.

Ferne House has long been demolished and Rushmore Lodge is now Sandroyd School, but these latterday alterations are ignored by the little signpost that you may pass if you follow the course of the

Roman road from Ashmore to Ludwell. In one direction an arm indicates simply 'Rushmore' and its companion 'Ferne'. In 1880 nothing more needed to be said.

It should not have taken long for the Fox-Pitts to learn that they had contemporaries living at Ferne. Sir Thomas Grove had at this time six children – two sons and four daughters. The two eldest daughters were already married. The two youngest girls do not easily yield precise information about their ages but they may be assumed to be no more than two or three years older than Agnes. The two sons were ten years apart, Walter being born in 1852 and Thomas in 1862. The news that old lord Rivers had died and that a host of young Fox-Pitts had arrived at Rushmore must have been received with enthusiasm at Ferne. At the least it meant a wider selection of partners at dances and lawn tennis parties. They were keen on such things at Ferne. The two youngest girls – Charlotte and Kathleen or 'Kat' – had formed their own ladies' tennis club with two of their cousins. As was the custom in those early days of the game they had designed their own club uniform, a playing costume decorated with the appropriate emblem of a frond of fern.

The mounting magnetic pull between the two houses is easily imagined. In September 1880 the visitors' book at Ferne was inscribed with the signature of St. George Fox-Pitt. This may be considered a preliminary reconnaissance by one of Agnes's elder brothers. In the following January the names of three more of the family appeared in the book. Alice and Lionel were there. And with them was 'Agnes G. Fox Pitt'.

Chapter Three

Rushmore was not the only new home to which Agnes had to accustom herself. The family's London address was no longer in Penywern Road, Earls Court. They were now to live in altogether grander style at 4 Grosvenor Gardens, in the fashionable district between Buckingham Palace and Sloane Square. Knightsbridge and Hyde Park soon became familiar scenes in everyday life, as did the smart shops of Brompton and Kensington. To ride in Rotten Row was as easy and delightful as to ride in Rushmore Park. The General and his family divided their time between town and country most agreeably, as their pleasures and their interests dictated.

From Agnes's point of view the house in Grosvenor Gardens was particularly well placed geographically because it was so close to Eaton Square. Number Fifty-one, Eaton Square was the town house of the Groves, which meant that the contact established between Rushmore and Ferne could be fortified and continued between 4 Grosvenor Gardens and 51 Eaton Square. With discretion, of course.

In July 1881 Agnes received a note from Eaton Square which indicated the stratagem that Walter Grove had in mind. She was known to him at this period, incidentally, by her second name.

My dear Miss Geraldine,

Do write me a line if you are going to ride in the Park tomorrow, and what time; as I should so like to ride the same time. So do write to me like a dear. My family went off today –

to Windsor. I went down to Newmarket today, got up at 7 A.M. Wasn't that good –

I liked your ball last night because you were kind to me and spoke to me severall times.

You are very nice indeed.

Though he might not be the most eloquent of lovers Walter was inventive in devising pretexts for their meetings away from Mama's watchful eyes. To synchronise their riding times was one way to engineer a chance encounter. Another was set out with shameless candour in a second letter.

My dear Miss Geraldine,

I have asked Mrs Pitt Rivers and party whom you doubtless know to lunch tomorrow. But if you can persuade her not to come, and come yourself with the P.B. or one of your brothers and sisters to accompany you, it would be so nice. I find I can't go to Mrs. Beaufoy's Tuesday as I'm going to a water party that day. You are very nice.

The identity of 'the P.B.' remains a mystery. The initials may represent 'Pleydell Bouverie.' A friend of this period is referred to frequently as 'Boob' or 'Booby', which sounds like an affectionately playful version of Bouverie. The Beaufoys were Wiltshire neighbours and political allies of the Groves. They lived at Donhead Hall, Donhead St. Mary in the 1880s – close to Ferne – and Mark Beaufoy became MP for Kennington.

The plot to bring Agnes Geraldine to Sunday lunch at Eaton Square, unaccompanied by her mother, misfired. There was apparently some confusion over the time at which the Pitt-Rivers party was expected to arrive. Next day a disappointed Walter wrote a humorously distraught letter of reproach.

51 Eaton Square,
S.W.

Monday night.

My dear Miss Geraldine –

I cannot say how grieved and disappointed I was at not seeing you my dear on Sunday it was insolent (to use that Lane

> Fox expression) to say the least of it of that mother of yrs not coming at the proper lunch hour and then running away and taking you off with her. Booby and I walked back here directly after Church and after being here for ½ an hour we walkd to yr house not knowing wether you were coming or not, And there a knocked kneed silly looking footman in the gordeous Pitt Rivers livery told us that, the whole family had gone off to lunch he didn't know where, I thought you had all gone off somewhere out of London altogether, So Booby and I forth with sat down on the pavement and sobbed as if our hearts would break till the gutters ran with our tears and after putting dust on our heads and put peas in our boots we went, for a stroll. It is a fearful sight to see two strong men weep; When we returned we found alas that you had come and gone. We then beat the butler sorely till he cried on his knees for mercy. Discharged the cook, put the rest of the servants on board wages for life Kicked the footman down stairs, threw the cat out of the window tore our respective hairs and took the first train for Richmond, so you see what sorrow yr mother brought into a household where all hitherto was peace. I'm off to a water party at 11.0 clock tomorrow. Are you going to Mrs. Roe's ball on Wednesday or are you going to ride Wednesday or going to Roehampton? You are so nice I should so much like to see you again, There seems so little chance of ever seeing you again. So do let me know yr Wednesday movements, If you are thinking of going to Roehampton I would go too.

'Insolent' was evidently a joke-word between them: it figured prominently in Agnes's vocabulary. Walter's destination at Richmond was probably the home of his eldest sister, Grace. Her husband, Hervey John de Montmorency, had died after only six years of marriage. She was usually referred to by Agnes as 'mrs. de Mont'.

Walter's three letters provide a useful first impression of his character and the way his courtship began. Although he was eleven years older than Agnes he was less articulate, more ingenuous and slower-witted. As a lover he seldom rises above the boyish level of 'You are very nice'. His easygoing goodnatured temperament held out a promise of repose and stability to her fiery, demanding spirit in its restless moods. His years at Eton had not fitted him for any particular role in life. He had vague political aspirations, but he was well content with the life of a country gentleman. Hunting, shooting and riding were his main preoccupations.

Agnes, even at eighteen, was already a more complex and high flying personality, with an intellectual background that belied the modest scope of her formal education. Her father did not suffer fools gladly and his ceaselessly enquiring mind must have influenced her. Even more so did the celebrated examples of her Stanley aunts and her Stanley grandmother. The Dover Street salon of the dowager Lady Stanley, widow of a Cabinet Minister, was famous for its sharp-tongued wit; and she herself was a campaigner for women's rights. Aunt Kate had married the son of Lord John Russell and was the mother of Bertrand. Aunt Rosalind was a well known public speaker, campaigning in the cause of Temperance. The word *campaigner* attaches itself easily to the Stanley women. Agnes's favourite aunt, Maude, started the first clubs for girls in London and campaigned for better educational opportunities for women. To grow up in the Stanley *milieu* was to be involved in the intellectual and political ferment of the period. In due time Agnes was to carry on that campaigning tradition.

In the summer and autumn of 1881, however, she was preoccupied with the more personal concerns of any eighteen-year-old, adventuring into romance and love, chafing at the restrictions of parental control, revelling in the pleasures and excitements of the adult world that she was beginning to enter with mounting confidence – the fashionable balls, the impromptu parties, the more sophisticated clothes, the first love-letters. It was all very different from the circumstances of that schoolgirl's diary of two years ago.

Her next diary – the next to survive, at least – resumes her narrative at the end of 1881. It is a journal rather than a diary, a stout notebook with a brass lock. With no printed daily divisions it gave her the freedom to write as much or as little as she pleased in each entry. It covers the extraordinarily tempestuous period before her marriage when she was under great strain: in moments of despair and loneliness she made the book her confidante.

The first entry relates to the Christmas period. On Boxing Day she hunted in traditional style with her brothers, Alex, Lionel and Douglas. The Groves were out with the hounds also. They all lunched at Ferne. Later in the day, at Rushmore, they gathered round the Christmas tree – an event which Agnes described as 'Rather slow but for talking to Walter who had been rather nice at

Ferne when we went in to luncheon'. The next day she went to the Blandford ball, which she enjoyed immensely. Walter gave her some flowers. She had nothing else to add concerning the last days of 1881 except a dismissive statement for which no reason is given: 'I was a fool'.

With the dawning of 1881 she apparently made a resolution to be accountable for every hour of her day, to fill each passing moment with useful and praiseworthy activities. The first of January was a disappointment, 'No visits all day,' she wrote, 'No New Year's festivities nor presents!' But next day she really got into her stride with the following entry.

> 2nd Monday. 9-10 Prayers, breakfast. 10-11 Practising and seeing others off riding. 11.10-12.15 Reading in my room, my hour, and mooning – thinking of Walter. Blaming myself really must not moon. 12-12.15 Still in my room, went down to drawing-room, pretended to read to Mama. Talked, about allowance. 1. Luncheon, still allowance, 2. Doctor came. 3. Went out driving in pony carriage with Mama. Went to see News, Rose, Bennett etc. gardener's wife, child ill. Drove rather badly till 4.30. Measured my room, talked to Douglas. 5. Wrote to Aunt Maud. Tea. 6. Talked to Alice about people coming here, and what she had done at Ferne. Walter wanted some girls – I thought quite natural. I could not dance with him the whole time. Went downstairs, came up again, went to workroom. Went to drawing room, talked about servants, wanted them sent away. 7 o'clock Dinner. After Dinner Mummers came, we all laughed. Still making a noise downs-stairs. 11.30 shan't be able to sleep. In the meantime I talked to Lionel – girls. Went and reread Aunt Maud's letter at 11.

It is a typical account of many similar days, starting with family prayers, taking in the charitable visits to family retainers, negotiating with parents for a better personal allowance and becoming absorbed in intimate gossiping with a brother or sister. Lionel was much preoccupied with girls in a flirtatious way, which inspired a sisterly protectiveness tinged with reproach in Agnes. Alice was in the closest confidence over Agnes's feelings for Walter. The morally stern but kindly influence of Aunt Maude was constantly felt by Agnes at this time. The other and growing influence was of course Walter Grove. There was as yet no commitment and they both flirted rather selfconsciously with others, but the power of their mutual attraction was now undeniable.

The early days of January followed a similar pattern, with Agnes trying to keep 11.00 to midday as her private hour. Once, catching herself in the act of doing nothing particular, she exclaimed angrily '*Must*' make use of that spare time working for Aunt Maud'. And again, on another day, 'Must read all I have been missing, mean to do some work for Aunt Maud's poor'. A particularly memorable day began with a visit to Wilton to lunch with Lady Pembroke. Some other guests who came by train included Baroness von Hügel and 'the rich Mr. Morison'. In the evening there was a concert at Tollard at which Agnes and Alice played a piano duet, and Alice played solos, to 'much applause.'

Some evenings Agnes played billiards with Lionel and proudly recorded her winnings of sixpence or a shilling. But the great events were the dances, at Rushmore and at Ferne, even though Walter missed the one given by Lionel at Rushmore. Somewhat to her surprise Agnes noted 'Enjoyed myself very much, thought I should not at first when they told me Walter was not coming – wonder why he didn't! They said his leg was bad. However, got on very fairly without him – dance a great success, I think everyone enjoyed themselves. L went away with Grace F. caused commotion'.

Grace F. must surely have been Grace Farquharson. Does L. represent Agnes's brother, Lionel? Grace caused an even greater commotion a few months later by running away with a married man.

The dance at Ferne was held the following night, Walter's leg being miraculously restored for the occasion. Agnes's verdict – 'Perfect bliss! Danced very often with the Napier boy and Walter. Went up to gallery with Walter for one or two dances. Fools made a commotion, I got angry but it was well worth it. I felt angry with him though I l. him. Napier was insolent'.

She had never before come so near to confessing 'I love him'. The refusal now to spell out the word, the limiting of it to the bare initial only, was perhaps an emotional precaution and at the same time a delight in keeping a lingering secret. One could still pretend that 'l' was short for 'like'. It took a further fortnight of visits for luncheon or dinner and quiet strolls together before she could write

> Walter and I became greater and more open friends than ever. This should be the happiest day of my life because I love Walter with all my heart.

Chapter Four

By the end of January, 1882, it would have been obvious to both families that Agnes and Walter were rapidly approaching the moment when they would want to make a formal announcement of their engagement. To the onlooker, and more particularly to the modern reader, it must seem an occasion for unalloyed rejoicing. Here were these two great families, whose broad acres marched side by side, now faced with the prospect of a firmer alliance than mere neighbourliness. It hardly seems fanciful to picture the two fathers shaking hands in cordial and mutual congratulation, while the mother of the bride-to-be weeps tears of gladness.

But life was not like that in the great dynastic households in 1882. There was the elaborate ritual of the marriage settlement to be undertaken, with all its legal and financial implications. Love might be a very agreeable element in such negotiations but it was no substitute for common sense and family interests. The firm judgement of parents had sometimes to bear down severely on the impulsiveness of their children. In short, neither General Pitt-Rivers nor Sir Thomas Grove responded with the unqualified delight that an ingenuous mind might have anticipated.

It is therefore necessary at this point to look more closely at the parents. Let us take the General first. He had to consider the welfare of nine children. His eldest daughter, Ursula, was already married and his three eldest sons were in some measure already established in their adult lives. Alex was destined to inherit Rushmore, as the General's heir. St. George, an independent spirit, had left home to make his own way as an inventor and businessman. Willy had joined the General's old regiment, the Grenadier Guards, and had already seen active service in the Zulu War in 1879. The five younger children were still wholly dependant, and the three boys seemed likely to remain so in the foreseeable future.

Where Agnes and Alice were concerned the General was prepared to give them, as married women, a personal allowance for life which spared them from being totally beholden to their husbands. Beyond that, he felt it his duty to make quite sure that a proposed husband could provide a suitable home and style of life for a daughter of the General and for any children of the marriage. In the case of Walter Grove the General wanted a positive commitment, and not a mere promise, on two points. There must be a stated and approved annual allowance paid to Walter by his father, during Sir Thomas's lifetime: and a guarantee that, after Sir Thomas's death, Ferne would pass intact to Walter as the eldest son. Those were the conditions to be met before the General would give his consent. In the circumstances they do not seem unreasonable.

Sir Thomas Grove, however, had other ideas. As the story unfolds it becomes clear that the financial substance of the Groves, outwardly so solid in appearance, was already flawed and fissured within. For one thing, the electoral expenses for winning and defending Sir Thomas's seat in Parliament were heavy. His London establishment in Eaton Square was costly, and so was his other establishment at Weymouth which he used when he went sailing in his yacht. It was not his way to deny himself anything that a gentleman might reasonably ask of life.

When his thoughts turned to marriage he saw clearly what might be achieved by that means. Having lost his wife in 1879 Sir Thomas was actively pursuing a wealthy widow who would consider his title and social position a fair exchange for her fortune. And what was good enough for himself, he reasoned, should be good enough for his son and heir. When Walter was ready to take a wife he should consider none but an heiress. Younger daughters, such as Agnes Geraldine Fox Pitt, were not to be taken seriously. All they could bring with them to the altar was pin money – a mere two or three hundred a year.

In the opening week of February Agnes's entries in her journal show the first signs of alarm. This is what she wrote

February 1st. Wednesday. Miserable day. Did not see Walter

in morning. Letter from Sir T. to Papa. Very unsatisfactory. Wrote to Walter, said we could not come to luncheon. No news of them all day. Felt I loved him better than anything. Only I do wish he would write.

2nd Thursday. Prayers. Letter from Kat. Such a nice one. Went to Wardour to luncheon, on way left letter for Kat at Ferne. On way back from Wardour went to Ferne. Walter gave me a letter he had written. Would not at first but I made him. Read letter when I got home. Oh such a heavenly dear kind beautiful letter. I felt I had never really loved him till then. Wrote a long one in return.

3rd Friday. They wanted me to write to Sir Thomas but I do not think I will. *No.*

4th Saturday. Beautiful warm day. Sun out, frost in morning. Afternoon rode to Ferne with Willy. Came home. Papa asked me where I had been. Then came up and spoke to me in Alice's room. Said he couldn't give me any more. Hope tomorrow's interview with Sir Thomas will be satisfactory. Have my misgivings. So sorry for my poor darling – fretting himself ill.

5th Sunday. Went to Tollard church, found Walter already there. Walked part of the way home with him. did not go into the house, stayed in the conservatory. Bliss! After luncheon he talked to Papa. No results – it was decided it must be off. I felt miserable but could hardly realise it. Then we went into the hothouse and talked there till past 5. Then I came in and cut off my hair and wrote to him as he asked me. Then I felt simply wretched, I would not go to tea of course. Mama came in. Passed a miserable night. Thinking of him and being separated from him.

The 'heavenly dear kind beautiful letter' that Walter had been reluctant to hand to her that Thursday afternoon was preserved by her and now makes a suitable companion-piece to set beside the pages of her journal:

'My dearest Geraldine,

I was too miserable to answer yr letter at once, and besides I wanted to see Sir T if he would do any more for me. However he said he couldn't give me more than £400 a year at present and as the General *only* gives £200 per annum to his daughters on marriage, Marriage on £600 a year would be simply impracticable, wouldn't it. He also said that these aunts from whom he will get an addition to his income of £1400 a year are only 88 and 89, may live some years, and as you say, long engagements are simply atrocious. So it must be *NO*, and the Darling Geraldine must be the Good Miss Agnes.

I really wish I had never spoken to you, but waited; but then I shouldn't have seen so much of yr. character and known what a true tenderhearted brave little woman you were, and what a treasure you are.

I shall not see you again till May most likely as you will be away in London and I shall be away. When you come down at Easter we can meet then (as meet we must not unfrequently living so near one another and with so many mutual friends) as trusted friends. It makes it easier for one when one thinks that one will see one another again, don't it?

Here we are disengaged then, at liberty to marry any one one pleases – I Jane, you the barman or the ostler. You have no idea how much better a person you have made me feel since I've known you. I will send you a sovereign by Kat I owe you. Will you keep it as a lucky one? I will daily pray it may bring you luck. Will you pray likewise I may obtain the great wish of my life. God bless you darling, don't be quarrelsome, as you have lately tried not to be, for when I hear of you from yr. brothers and sisters it will make me so happy to hear of you as the sweet angel who has shed so bright a light across my path.

Goodbye dear love – although *that* no more must I call you. Yet the recollections of you are so sweet to think on. So on that I live, with great hopes for the future. God bless you, my child, and goodbye: He will bless you as you deserve it, you are so good.

Ever yrs. faithful –

Walter.

It was perhaps characteristic of him that he should crumble under the first rebuff and adopt the traditional attitudes of a gentleman doing the honourable thing. He was always a gallant loser. Agnes was made of sterner stuff and in a different tradition. Her father had been flatly rejected by Lord Stanley as a suitor for Alice Stanley;

but he had married her in the end, nevertheless. The 'quarrelsomeness' that Walter had already discerned in Agnes was evidence of her determination not to be put down in a conflict of wills.

The immediate prospect was that the parents would want to terminate the relationship without unseemly acts of rupture. The sanctions, hidden from the public eye, were to make Walter no longer a welcome visitor to Rushmore and to frown on any correspondence between the lovers – or even positively to forbid it. To all this Agnes's response was ingenious. She was touched by Walter's act of noble renunciation, but not influenced by it. Letters continued to pass between them, using Agnes's sister, Alice, and Walter's sisters, Charlotte and Kate, as go-betweens where necessary; but an even better form of communication occurred to Agnes when she resolved to send her journal to Walter. The idea came to her soon after she had left Rushmore and gone to London. She drew a line between the last day at Rushmore and the first in London and wrote beside it 'This is where it began to be meant for you – the rest not.' In future her entries would be intended for Walter to read. Even better than an exchange of letters they would exchange journals from time to time. A second book was to be started by Walter so that they could take turn and turn about. The plan was to synchronise each exchange of volumes, to read the latest entries made by the other writer and then to add new daily entries until the next exchange was due. As a substitute for direct letterwriting it was highly effective.

Back in London, at Grosvenor Gardens, Agnes unpacked her private ornaments and thought about Walter. She had hoped to see him at Tisbury station before she left but he was not there. London was foggy and horrid; she missed the beautiful country air and awoke next morning with a headache. Her first outing was to Dover Street to confide in the redoubtable Aunt Maude, who approved of Walter. Gratefully Agnes noted,

> When I said he was sorry he had said anything she said – "Oh no, I am very glad he proposed! It's much better." We were then interrupted by the entrance of the grandmother, who said she was sorry but felt all would come right like my dear Walter himself says. He must know best so I am bright and hopeful too.

Aunt Maude's support was invaluable at this stage. Next day she took

Agnes for a ride in her carriage, to call on Aunt Margaret and Florence.

> Aunt Maude stopped them short in a flow of congrats whereupon began a stream of condolences, but with positive assurances that all would come well. Aunt Maude had said, when she heard of it first "But I suppose he writes to you every day?" Perhaps he does in a way! Who knows? But when I told her, No, she said "Well, perhaps better not." Then we went to Covent Garden Market, and then to see some poor people. Aunt M would not drive up to their door because she said it would look ostentatious!

During her first week in London Agnes seemed eager to immerse herself in a busy round of activities. Some mornings she spent three hours at the Grosvenor School of Art. Afternoons might include a visit to the Royal Institution to hear a lecture on 'The Senses' or 'Corals'. At any time there might be visits to or from friends and relations. The entries in her journal are tightly compressed and peppered with names – some unidentified but others worth mentioning as being of more than passing interest.

A fellow student at the art-school was one of Agnes's cousins, Marie Adeane, who later became a maid of honour to Queen Victoria. Another cousin frequently mentioned at this time was Marcia – otherwise 'Mushie' – daughter of Sackville George Lane Fox, who in 1859 had succeeded his uncle as Baron Conyers. After his death Marcia became Lady Conyers in her own right, and in 1886 she married the Earl of Yarborough. Thomas Hardy wrote an amusing description of her in his autobiography where he identified her as the lady in his poem *The Pretty Pink Frock*. Then there was Madame Novikov, a Russian lady journalist who enjoyed the friendship of Gladstone and Campbell-Bannerman; and Mrs. Bontine who told Agnes that her son, Charley Graham, was going to be married to Miss B – 'a lovely girl, they say, and a friend of the Prince of Wales! and on less than £*700* a year!!!'

No wonder Agnes was startled by this last bit of gossip. If such a marriage could be launched on so slender an income there must be hope for her and Walter. And in spite of her almost feverish activity there were quiet times when thoughts of Walter absorbed her.

> I spent from 6 to 7 alone with Walter today. Sweet communings of my own heart and his in the spirit. I wonder whether he is thinking of me! Perhaps! Oh yes there is affinity of spirit between those who love one another.

Perhaps Mrs. Pitt-Rivers hoped that the excitements of the London season, the natural ebullience of youth and the attentions of other and more eligible young men would distract Agnes. What, for instance, might be the effect of a ballroom meeting with one of Agnes's earlier 'crushes' – Lord Carlow's son, say, young Dawson Damer?

> In the evening we went to the Halfords' ball but although I enjoyed it immensely because I danced and it was fun and the people were appreciative(!) and above all because I could look at Dawson Damer, still I thought I loved my own more than ever and I did yearn oh so much for my darling to come to me. Oh won't he? I think my yearning is more intense than anything.

That she was not overdramatising her 'yearning' became clear next day when Walter's sister, Kat, came to stay at Grosvenor Gardens. In the evening Mrs. Pitt-Rivers and Alex went to dinner with Lady Stanley and Maude at Dover Street. The three girls, Agnes, Alice and Kat, had dinner at home. After dinner Alice wrote a 'rather inane' letter to Walter, and Agnes talked to Kate.

> I felt that I loved Kathleen passionately and we were lying on the sofa together and I simply hugged her and felt oh so in love with her and I found out after it was only Walter I was thinking of the whole time! – that I was yearning longingly for him. But of course I do love K too for her own sake and especially because she's his sister and more especially because she is his favourite. Oh I do, at this moment I am writing, long inexpressibly to see to hear to feel my Walter's presence.

Chapter Five

By the end of February 1882 the atmosphere at 4 Grosvenor Gardens was distinctly tense; sudden emotional storms became frequent. The male part of the household tended to come and go in the intricate pattern of separate individual lives, so that one never knew who might be there on any particular day – with Alex not yet back from Vienna, Willy attending his duties in the Guards, Arthur and Douglas appearing and disappearing, the General somewhat remote from domestic matters. The constant and explosive factor was the three women, Agnes, Alice and their mother.

For Mrs. Pitt-Rivers it was a difficult time. Alice was now twenty, Agnes eighteen and a half, and any mother might have found them a handful to manage: they were rebellious, excitable and wilful to a degree. In the best of circumstances they would have found parental discipline difficult to bear. The frustration of Agnes's hopes for a speedy marriage made an otherwise difficult situation totally intolerable. The clash between parents and children at times took on the character of open warfare.

It was the General's role to be drawn in as the ultimate authority: the day-to-day frictions concerned Mrs. Pitt-Rivers whose duty was to keep the girls under control. One is tempted to sympathise with her, although she can hardly be considered a sympathetic character. Her most celebrated attribute was her meanness. In his description of breakfast at Rushmore Bertrand Russell recounted how his aunt had become a miser –

> and if visitors left any of their bacon and egg she would put it back in the dish. One of her sons was a Guardsman, very smart and correct. He always came down late for breakfast and rang the bell for fresh food. When he ordered it, my Aunt would scream at the footman, saying there was no need of it as there was plenty left from the scrapings from the visitors' plates.

She was also reputed to return to the dining room after dinner to recover any wine left in the glasses, until some practical joker surreptitiously topped up the glasses with vinegar.

Her own adolescence had been difficult and wearisome under an autocratic father whose intransigeance nearly prevented her marriage. Did she perhaps feel, in some obscure way, that it was no more than a sort of rough justice that Agnes should suffer as she had done? In her memory must have rankled the tart comments of her mother and grandmother, who disparaged her so tirelessly in their letters to each other: 'Poor Alice – does anything amuse *her*? Was she ever very amusable?' Two years after her presentation to the Queen at a Drawing room in 1846 – 'I am afraid you will be obliged to bring her again to Town without a husband'. And three years later 'I do wish Alice had a good husband of some kind or other.'

The irony was that the man she eventually married in 1853 had proposed in 1849 and been rejected on financial grounds by her parents, who were extremely angry later when Major Lane Fox wrote to Alice without their permission. The state of affairs between Agnes and Walter was no novelty to Mrs. Pitt-Rivers. She had lived through it all thirty years earlier, bearing her frustration with patience. Perhaps that is why she now appeared to act equivocally, at times nettled by the vehemence of Agnes's protests, at other times almost encouraging Walter not to despair. Nor is vehemence too strong a word for the outbursts that Agnes committed to her journal in the account of her rows with 'The Man' and 'The Minor One' as she now dubbed her parents.

> February 23. Had a row with that insolent maid. Sorry – not my fault. Tea – rows. Rowy day. I felt miserable.
>
> Feb. 26, Sunday. Alice went to church. I did not. They came back just as I was starting for Sunday School. Got abused for going. Shameful.
>
> Feb. 27. Late for breakfast, considerable disturbance. I got *very* angry. Really angry. With the Man too. Went to drawing

class. Did panels etc. Came home. Felt better after I had sympathised with Alice. Much.

Feb. 28. I did not go to the lecture because I should have had to go alone in the carriage with the Man as far as Mortimer House, and as he had been very disagreeable to both Alice and I we both refused to go.

March 1st. Drawing till one, then I went to see Edith S dressed for the Drawingroom. Then after luncheon Alice and I (and Doug) wanted to go to Barkers, and Mama said she did not *choose* us to go. We said we would as we were not babies to be ordered about like rats. So the Man joined in and swore like anything at Alice. *Of course* I took Alice's part so he began on me, so we went out of the room when it was over, straight to Barker's. Then I ordered a gown and different things and then we came back – a gloomy dinner! Poor Alice – I have a faint chance of escape from this tyranny and misery but she seems to have none as yet, but I am certain Providence could not in justice allow her to go on much longer in this place. I only wish, oh so much, that my fate could be decided.

2nd. I arranged my room till the dressmaker came and then there was a row about *that*. It's so degrading – fancy not being allowed to order what one likes. Then Kathleen came. I was *so* glad to see her of course. And she is going to write to me about the race in which Walter was riding. I do hope and trust that it will be what it ought to be. It's so nice seeing K. It reminds me of him. She left about 3. After tea Mama came and tried to lecture me! We did not go to the Speaker's in the evening because of Aunt Rianette's death. She left Aunt Maud £4000. If only someone would die and leave me some.

3rd. Post card from Charlotte and letter from Kathleen telling me of my dear friend's success. I was oh so delighted. I came and told everyone downstairs. Alex was very jealous! and said it was all the horse. I had a row in the afternoon because Mama said she would not take me to the play on account of my 'conduct'. I wished to know what conduct. However, Alice and I did not go and what's more we had to have our dinner upstairs. More fun. In the evening I was so delighted and excited and mad with joy. A letter to Alice from dear Walter saying he would be in London on Saturday.

It was all a failure, I can't write about it. It makes me cry now.

What happened on Saturday was that Walter picked the wrong moment to call. Alice was at home but Agnes was out. She had spent the morning at the art-school, drawing an almond sprig in blossom. When the session was over she refused a lift from Marie Adeane, intending to be alone in case Walter met her in the street. He had still not appeared when the time came for her to go to a lecture with Mrs. Pitt-Rivers. After the lecture, she wrote, 'I was so tantalized because Mama drove about all over the place and I was wanting to get home and see if –' but, alas, she was too late. Walter had called and departed. To think of having been so near, yet missing him, was more than she could bear.

After this disappointment family life calmed down briefly and Agnes continued her journal rather listlessly, except when Colonel Digby called and pleased her by saying 'Great thing, Walter Grove winning this point-to-point'. A week later the domestic strife was resumed.

> March 11. Grand row. The Man swore etc. I had dinner up in my sitting-room.
> March 12. I came down to breakfast. It began again so I was very angry but restrained myself which made him more angry. Oh the misery of these two days. I shall never forget.

On the following day the General departed to Rushmore. Meanwhile there had been some secret moves, involving Aunt Maude and Kathleen Grove, to make a fresh opportunity for Walter to see Agnes in London. After the previous fiasco Agnes had written to him, congratulating him – and his horse, Harboro' – on the point-to-point victory, and telling him about Aunt Maude's legacy from Great-aunt Rianette. There had also been a note of reproach in her letter to judge from his reply –

> My dear child
>
> I'm enclosing this by yr mother, I hope she will give it you. I'm sure she wont prosper if she dont. Will she. It is too awful not being able to write to you every day, and hear from you. Oh how I do wish that Grovie would get married to that widow quick, its dreadful work waiting especially as one is not engaged and can't see one another or even I can't write to you. What wouldn't I give to see you once more even if I didn't have

a chance of speaking to you. I intend going up to London next week for a day or two. I shall then see you riding in the park or walking or somehow or other and then I shall return here, and live in the thoughts of having seen you looking well and happy. I'm afraid I've really fallen in love with you my darling, fancy that, and to think that I'm not engaged to marry you nor you engaged to me and that we may not see or write to each other, loving one another as much as we do (I can answer for my part) simply because we've got stingy parents – it's too annoying. And Grovie's marriage is really our only hope for the present. I daily pray for it. Grovie writes to her almost every day and has hardly missed a week without going up to London. You will see, when he does get married he won't tell anyone till just before hand, as he would hate an engagement for more than a month; don't you think so yrself?

I'm glad you were pleased at my winning that Point to Point race the other day. I simply imagined I saw you at the winningpost so of course I got there first. You don't know how disappointed I was at not seeing you in London the other day I would have given years of my life to have just seen you for a moment. I never, never, was so annoyed about anything before in all my life.

I am carving my old Eton bureau and have made a most ornamental production of it. I intend it for the corner of yr boudoir some day, when you come and stay with me forever. It is rather amusing work carving and keeps one out of mischief when one has nothing to do, as I frequently have now since I've taken to economising and staying at home so much.

Kathleen told me you and Alice had made up yr. minds to treat the General's impertinances with the silent contempt they deserve. I bet two to one you don't my darling. You are far too much of a pepperpot to bear unpleasant remarks in silence.

Hunting will be over very early this year as everything is so forward. Such crowds of primroses everywhere, the farmers won't like their young wheat and grass fields ridden over so there won't be much hunting after the end of March.

It was horrid of you saying in yr. letters to me that I prefer waiting in uncertainty to marrying at once. As you know, you would not be allowed to marry me on six or seven hundred a year. I would marry you on 800 a year gladly, but I know my father and yrs would neither of them consent to it and we are both entirely dependant on them.

What's to be done? It's most annoying, but my hope is in Mrs. Fenwick. She has £5000 a year for two or three years and will have 3000 then as two of it is allowed her to keep her son till he's of age. Now do send me a line by your mother and tell me what chance I have of seeing you. If you post a letter Sunday night I get it by second post at half past four on Monday. The end or middle of the week would be most convenient to me to be in London.

I wish I knew Aunt Maud. I'm sure I should so much like to, as she is so kind and nice to you. Have you many balls next week – are there any I could go to, to see you?

Mrs. Fenwick was the widow to whom Sir Thomas was currently paying his attentions. It was Walter's hope that his father would secure the lady and her fortune, and would then be able and willing to give Walter a sufficient allowance to leave Ferne and set up his own establishment – with Agnes as his wife, of course. Few stepmothers can have been so eagerly awaited as the future Lady Grove, whoever she was to be, provided she brought wealth with her.

Walter's visit to London took place on March 14, with no apparent encouragement from Mrs. Pitt-Rivers. On the previous day there were some rapid exchanges of signals, by note and by telegram, in which Aunt Maude and Kat were involved, immediately after the General's departure to Rushmore. Next day Agnes went to lunch at 35 Dover Street, and from there on to Number 40, where Lady Stanley and Aunt Maude lived. 'Strangely enough', she wrote in her journal, 'to my joy Walter at the door!' She then went on to the Royal Institution, where Walter came in and sat beside her.

Next day, after her morning session at the art-school, she found Walter waiting to walk back with her. This proved to be too indiscreet. Agnes 'got into a row because that horrible maid told'. It was clearly one of the hazards of life in the Pitt-Rivers household, as in many another such, that the servants engaged in domestic espionage and probably counter-espionage as well. Agnes was now paying for the luxury of her earlier rebuke to this 'insolent' maid.

For a week Walter remained in London, seizing any opportunity for a meeting. He wrote to Alice, to make an assignation in Hyde

Park. Agnes recounted how she and Alice 'went up Grosvenor Place by ourselves and tremblingly into the Park'. No sooner did they meet Walter than Alice's dog, Bogie, ran away and Walter had to chase after it. They met again in the Park next day, and at church on Sunday Walter came and sat beside her. The next night Agnes was invited to a ball at the Halford's and Walter had contrived to be invited too. In her journal Agnes wrote 'Greatly enjoyed – truly pleasurable! Walter so nice, Came home with us in carriage. Last I saw of him. Poor me! Poor he!'

While he was in London Walter spent some time with Agnes's brother, St. George, and it was perhaps at this time that St. George began to outline a plan that he developed in more detail later, to overcome the financial obstacle that prevented Agnes and Walter from marrying. St. George was a quixotic and generous character, whom Bertrand Russell considered to be the most interesting of the family, saying of him –

> He was one of the first inventors of electric light, but he threw up all such things for esoteric Buddhism and spent his time travelling in Tibet to visit mahatmas. When he returned, he found that Edison and Swan were making electric lights which he considered an infringement of his patent. He thereupon entered upon a long series of lawsuits, which he always lost and which finally left him bankrupt. This confirmed him in the Buddhist faith that one should overcome mundane desires. My grandmother Stanley used to make him play whist, and when it was his turn to deal, she used to say, 'I'm glad it is your turn to deal, as it will take away your air of saintliness'. He combined saintliness and Company-promoting in about equal proportions.

In the case of Agnes's predicament St. George's idea was to find some form of employment for Walter which would provide a sufficient income. To do this was not so easy as it might seem. Eton had not fitted Walter for a salaried career of any kind. He was now in his thirtieth year and does not appear to have had any sort of employment, not even in the running of the family estate. However, St. George was active in the commercial world, with companies of his own, and he decided to see what might be done to find a suitable job for Walter. Russell's malicious gibe at St. George's combination of saintliness and company-promotion was no more than the truth on this occasion.

For Agnes March ended in relative calm. Walter's letters, addressed conspiratorially to Alice, were getting through. She also received the first instalment of the journal she had persuaded him to keep. This was in a large and awkwardly shaped book that they soon discarded. His second episode forms the beginning of a smaller volume. On March 30th Agnes notes 'All morning I read my Walter's book'. She then closed her journal and sent it to Walter. In the following week she left London and returned with the family to Rushmore.

Chapter Six

April was a calmer and happier month for Agnes. She was back at Rushmore for Easter and with the connivance of the sisters – Alice and the two Grove girls, Kat and Charlotte – it was not difficult to arrange meetings that looked casual enough. Walter had unfortunately to be away for part of the month, firstly on a visit to Lord and Lady Trafalgar at Chippenham and later to stay with friends in South Wales, but at such times the two journals were much used and passed to and fro successfully. The enthusiasm for these exchanges abated later, but in April there was a great outpouring of words in which their differing characters are clearly shown – with Walter being affectionate, humorous, pleasure-loving and submissive, while Agnes is altogether more intense and demanding. For the time being they both seemed content, for the most part, to accept the deadlock in their marriage plans and to enjoy the immediate delights of expressing their mutual love.

When Agnes posted away her journal at the end of March she addressed it to Bowden Hill, Chippenham, where it was handed to Walter in his bedroom early on a Sunday morning. Reading her account of the first three months of 1882 so absorbed him that he did not get down to breakfast until nearly eleven o'clock and had to rush off to church with Lady Trafalgar, without anything to eat. He was obviously moved by some of the earlier revelations of Agnes's love for him, but he could not resist the temptation to parody her literary style. There was always a streak of chaffing, satirical humour in Walter and in his first entry after hers he gave it full rein –

> Was given this diary in bed, don't know why didn't feel quite myself, got up, looked at myself in the glass have grown a mustache in the night. Something wrong, why did the footman call me? All I know is that Agnes G. Lane Fox Pitt is my name and I'm wildly in love with a dear sweet angelic darling little child, called Geraldine. But then somebody called me Walter at breakfast. Well I *am* mixed. Hope to be sorted some day, went upstairs, came down again and then asked the footman what wages he got, and if he'd got an aunt, and if chilblains were a joy to him, I really mustn't moon, mooning so bad for one, see. I'll go out and sun myself instead. Came in, had a slight disagreement with 'the man', blackened his right eye, knocked his left eye into the heel of his right boot, and left the room with dignity. Never lose yr. temper. Went upstairs. Augustine was insolent, caught her by the ear, she left the room hurriedly, her ear came off in my hand. Horrid ear to come off so. Now to bed. Goodnight.

As a lampoon it has its merits. 'See?' became a private catchword between them. And having had his joke Walter was quick to ask her to excuse this 'bosh', adding 'you don't mind my chaffing you, do you?' To this Agnes replied in a rather painstaking and humourless way, 'Simply, you horrid old thing, of course I put everything I do down in this, it's not meant to be interesting, not like a letter. In a diary one puts *all* one had done during the day – in a letter one only tells news and talks nonsense'.

From Chippenham Walter went to Dorchester where Albert Bankes and Sir Charles D'Oyly swore him in as a magistrate. Both men were well known to him as comparatively near neighbours. Bankes lived at Kingston Lacy, between Wimborne and Badbury Rings, and was a personal friend with whom Walter sometimes stayed. D'Oyly lived in the fine house at Iwerne Stepleton which had once been the home of Peter Beckford and Agnes's Pitt-Rivers ancestors. At the lunch after the swearing-in ceremony Walter met other magistrates and marvelled at the capacity of Teddy Portman, commenting 'I never saw anyone eat the quantity of mutton chops, it was like shovelling coals down into a London coal-cellar. He has plenty of stowage room certainly but still one began to think, where on earth does he put it all to?'

During his weekend at Chippenham Walter had written a letter to Agnes which indicated that St. George had made him an offer of some kind of employment. Encouraged by this he wanted to challenge the rule that forbade Agnes to write openly to him.

My own dear sweet darling child,

I have just got yr. letter. It's rubbish our not writing to one another. I am waiting every day to hear from St. George as I want so to know when I am to commence work as I'm rather anxious to begin. Do find out from him if I can and let me know. It's rubbish yr. not writing to me. I am perfectly determined to marry you, and you me, and it's a certainty to come off so why shouldn't you write to yr. future husband, See?

Why I'm waiting to hear from St. George before I speak to Sir Thomas is that it will have greater effect on him if I tell him that I've got a secretaryship and begin tomorrow, than that I've been promised one and don't know when I begin.

I shall take unfurnished rooms and furnish them. I've got a certain amount of furniture. I don't suppose I shall marry you before the winter as I shall have to work like a nigger at first and I want to get thoroughly accustomed to the work before I am married.

I fancy that Tommy is making for another widow. She is older than Mrs. Fenwick and has 3 old daughters. I don't think there is a chance of her marrying him. What a funny fellow he is.

The few days approaching Easter passed in uneventful happiness. Sometimes Agnes took Lionel with her as a chaperone and Kat accompanied Walter. If they went walking it was to a prearranged meeting-place. If they went riding they met and rode together. The woods were looking lovely in their first springtime greenery as Walter and Agnes cantered through the Chase on Easter Sunday – and then it was time for Walter to set off on his journey to Pembrokeshire. They had arranged for him to write to Alice three times during the week, and he tried to console Agnes for his absence with the thought that she would at least be spared any family rows, such as might be expected when he was in the vicinity of Rushmore.

Before Walter left they dismembered his first journal, 'so huge and cumbersome', and he took a new and smaller one to Wales. In this he chronicled his success and tribulations in various horse races and the little comedies and excitements of house parties and fancy dress balls. He was obviously having a whale of a time, doing what he was good at – mastering horses and beguiling women.

At Rushmore life was quieter. The main events seem to have been excursions to the Larmer Tree, where the General was developing his pleasure grounds. The tree itself was an ancient wych-elm: according to local tradition it had been a meeting place for King John's hunters, when the whole of Cranborne Chase was a royal hunting ground. John certainly owned the Chase for a time, after it came to him by marriage, and he hunted here on a number of occasions. The Larmer Tree was probably a recognised landmark on the boundary between Dorset and Wiltshire and could therefore have been a suitable meeting place, even if the association with King John were a later embellishment. The tree was certainly used in the eighteenth and early nineteenth centuries as the site for the annual Court Leet of the manor of Tollard on the first Monday in September, and it was from here that the Tollard Hunt started while the Court was in session.

All this was of obvious interest to General Pitt-Rivers. He examined the etymology of the word *Larmer* – inconclusively. He applied his archaeological techniques to what was known as King John's House and demonstrated that the earliest part of the building was constructed some years after John's death – a discovery which did not, however, inhibit the General two years later from describing the house as 'formerly a hunting box of King John'. Ancient traditions are not easily surrendered. As for the wych-elm itself – it was, alas, in a sorry condition when the General inherited it. What little remained was decayed and hollow, so a sapling oak was planted inside it and is destined to inherit the name. If you think of the oak as 'Lane Fox' and the wych-elm as 'Pitt-Rivers' it becomes a pretty piece of symbolism.

At the height of their fame the Larmer Grounds attracted tens of thousands of visitors each year and served several purposes. On the first Monday in September they provided a modern equivalent of the old festivities of the Tollard Hunt and Court Leet feast, in place of which the General provided races and athletic competitions, a concert and open-air dancing. For the local villagers the Larmer Grounds provided a social setting, where a band played and the habitual narrowness of their lives could be broadened a little. For the wider public the Grounds became a magnet, drawing them to the entertainment the General offered free of charge, but also to sample the instructive experience he provided in his nearby museum at Farnham. Popular education was the underlying purpose. In an address to the Society of Arts in 1891 he said, 'The knowledge of the facts of evolution, and of the processes of gradual development, is the one great knowledge we have to inculcate, whether in natural history or in the arts and institutions of mankind; and this knowledge can be taught by museums, provided they are arranged in such a manner that those who run may read. The working classes have but little time for study'. To bring the masses to his educational museum he had to devise what he called 'other inducements'. In 1890, the year before this address, The Larmer Grounds had attracted 16,839 visitors, and 7000 visited the Museum.

Such developments can hardly have been in the General's mind in 1880 when he started work on the Larmer Grounds. The Farnham Museum did not open till 1888, nor the art collection at King John's House till 1891, so it was not as an inducement to visit them that the temple was built at the Larmer Grounds in 1880 and the half-timbered cottage – in the *ferme ornée* manner – in 1881. Perhaps they were no more, in their inception, than the private follies that landowners of the period liked to construct. For the family it made a pleasant jaunt, to walk or ride over from Rushmore to take tea at the Larmer Grounds about a mile and a half away. Thus on Easter Monday, 1882, while Walter was in Wales, Agnes recorded that 'Kathleen came to luncheon and we all went to the Larmer Tree and had tea there. Great fun. Ali-boy, Lionel, Plonks, Alice and I. We saw Carry riding but he would not accept our kind invitation to come in and partake of our humble fare. Then we walked home and met the General and his spouse parading their newly acquired land and surveying the improvements'.

Nicknames were frequently coined and sometimes discarded quickly. Which of the group was called 'Plonks' for a while, I cannot guess – Douglas possibly. 'Carry' looks like a diminutive of 'Carrots', the nickname of Agnes's youngest brother, Arthur. Ali-boy was her eldest brother, Alex.

On the previous day the Larmer Grounds had had a weightier visit: 'In the afternoon Sir Thomas and Kathleen came. Sir Thomas and Papa went on to the Larmer Tree. We were afraid of their cart breaking down – I don't *think* it did, however'.

Agnes must have been greatly concerned to know what passed between the two men but her journal gives no precise information. What is noticeable, however, is that she seemed to incline to a more hopeful view of Walter's father.

> I can't help liking Sir Thomas somehow. I suppose because he's your father, but he is rather nice. He said to Kathleen about having said nothing to my good parents because there was nothing to say; and that if it could be managed he would be the last person to say anything against it, because I was rather a nice person – which of course no one can but admit! And so Kathleen said something about your wishing to try and do something, which Sir Thomas immediately pooh-poohed, but Kathleen says he cannot now be surprised if you ask him about something now.
>
> I feel rather sick at heart and a-weary of life at this present moment. I do get downhearted at intervals because I feel so helpless and I think if only *I* were a man, how different things would be. I would have long since quitted the paternal roof and wandered out alone like St. George has done, and made my fortune by some gigantic stroke of genius which is now pent up in my unfathomable brain and senselessly thrown away upon a female *woman*! Bah! I can't think why men are so fond of women. I can see nothing at all attractive in most of them. Anymore than I can see anything attractive for women in the generality of these nimminy-pimminy men that one sees. Can you? I like those ancient heroes who always had done something brave and were upright honest warlike men; but of course in these peaceable civilized times all that sort of thing has been given place to by bravery, not in shedding blood, but in fighting against the Power of Evil.

Warming to her task Agnes covered several more pages with a powerful sermon, commending virtue and high principle to Walter and assuring him of the reformative power of religion. What is so endearing about her is the way her moods of rather ponderous Victorian moralising suddenly break up, as on this occasion, into a sort of pirouetting gaiety –

> There is, there can be, no sham about real religion. Can there? I don't know how long I have been writing for but I do believe

> that for the few minutes I did forget self, and really and truly mean everything I say. I feel that if you are good, and me good, we shall be so much happier and we shall be able to trust each other so implicitly. I could never be jealous of anything you did because I should know that your duty and your principle, as well as your love for me, would prevent your doing anything I should not like, you wicked thing. You must not write to that horrid person who wanted to kick you. She can't be nice, or she wouldn't have wanted. Besides, she's a nasty horrid untruthful person to call herself *your* Elsie, because *I'm yours* so she can't be too. See?
>
> But *I'm* not jealous – if you think I am, you're most wonderfully mistaken. It's very lucky, if you care to hear all this, that I take it into my head to *write* it because we never *talk* anything but fearful nonsense when we get together. I wonder why – but one does write more seriously than one talks, as a rule. Well, if we wrote down some of the things that we talked, and showed it to any 3rd person, they would simply call a cab and have us both off to the nearest lunatic asylum.
>
> But now I must finish simply. Good night, dearest.

Walter got home from Wales little more than a day before Agnes was due to leave Rushmore. His successes as an amateur jockey had evidently encouraged him to stay longer than he at first intended or she expected. There was a deeper quarrel than the sudden little tiffs that could always flare up with Agnes's unpredictable temperament. His changes of address in Wales had confused the exchange of journals so that for a week Agnes had neither volume in which to confide her thoughts – and this had aggravated her impatience. As usual Walter bowed to the storm. He justified his absence in Wales as a means of sparing them both from the 'sneaking underhand' methods they would have had to employ to meet each other daily near Rushmore. 'You see', he explained, 'I am in such an unpleasant position as all the difficulty against the marriage is on my side (my father's side rather) and with somewhat doubtful prospects'. As for the sharply worded letters that reached him before he left Wales, he conceded –

> You are quite right as to yr. scolding me for my casual *laisser aller* indolence. That is indeed my besetting sin, there is no doubt it's a good deal constitutional. I'm afraid I shall never

> quite get rid of it entirely but I have always looked forward to you as my helper in that matter. Yr. energetic character and dear little flashes of temper will hustle and make me less indolent. I think the life I have led, simply pleasure seeking with no particular aim beyond getting through the time with as little trouble and with as much excitement as possible, rather conducive to indolent habits.

It was an honest self-assessment and it explains the general course of their future relationship, with Agnes as the pacemaker. But now, in the short time they had together there was much to talk about. Aunt Maude had suggested a job that might suit Walter, writing to Agnes 'Would he do for a factory inspector, I hear there are some going to be made, so do try and get one. That *can't* be hard'. Then there was news that one of the elderly Grove aunts was ill, and they could hardly help speculating on the money her death might bring to Sir Thomas. As they pondered these matters Walter presented himself openly at Rushmore, having considered that Mrs. Pitt-Rivers would know he had returned from Wales and had met Agnes, and would think them both underhand if he did not appear. Next day Agnes caught the London train, dejected that Walter was nowhere to be seen.

At Ferne he was making what was to be his final entry in either of the journals. That evening he too went to the railway station and departed.

Chapter Seven

Before he left Ferne, on Thursday April 27, 1882, Walter made a final entry in Agnes's original journal. He was going to stay with one of his married sisters, Edith Foster, at Clewer Manor near Windsor, breaking his journey in London overnight, and he intended to send the journal to Agnes at 4 Grosvenor Gardens by a messenger. The content of his entry was such as should please her.

> The poor old Aunt died this morning, so now I must have a great fight with Sir Thomas for you. I have arranged to go to London tonight and shall send this to you. I go down to Clewer tomorrow and shall write to Sir Thomas. One can do these sort of things with him better by writing because, if I talk to him, he always loses his temper and becomes unreasonable; and he begins to talk nonsense, and that always annoys me. He won't commit himself to write nonsense on paper, and any promise I can get out of him I shall have in black and white. See, darling?
>
> You did make me so miserable yesterday, yr. darling little face did look so inexpressibly sad, you poor dear. You gave me quite a shudder when you looked out of the window of the brougham. Why were you so sad, and I am myself full of hope. You see it is a case of now or never. I daren't think of the never.
>
> I will send you a copy of my letter to Sir Thomas and his answer etc. I will write tomorrow.

There again seems to have been some bungling in the handover of the journal. Agnes's first entries after Walter's are perfunctory and seem to have been written in retrospect. On the 30th she wrote 'I've missed several days in my consecutive diary but it's W's fault, with your careless dilatory ways of dealing with the books. Do you wish them gone on with?'

The answer, whether Walter gave it or not, was No. The next move would have been for Agnes to send the smaller second book to Walter at Clewer, and it might be expected that she would have been making entries in it up to the 27th or 28th. However it contains nothing after the 23rd when she wrote an astonishingly bitter and angry outburst occasioned by Walter's prolongation of his Welsh visit. First she had expected him to return on a Wednesday, then on Sunday, then Monday – and finally he arrived late on Tuesday, knowing that she might by then have already left Rushmore. 'You will not see this', she wrote, declaring also her intention never to write another letter to him. And she wound up her passionately vituperative denunciation with a bravura display of hurt pride –

> You really mustn't think I am a scrap more anxious to see you than you are to see me. You are not worth anything. Please don't think I care more than you – I am only disappointed. No, not even that – I'm angry at having been given the trouble. No, it's not that. I am not anything – only I don't care a bit. Yes I do though, because I hate to find people, anyone, even the kitchen maid, not true and honest. That's it. It's for humanity's sake, that's all – not you individually.

Did she perhaps decide, on reflection, that she preferred not to send the journal at this point for Walter to read her impassioned condemnation before continuing to make his entries? Or was the novelty of the exchange of journals wearing thin, and were the delays and mislayings cancelling any benefits? Whatever the reason Agnes retained the principal journal as its only author henceforth and the subsidiary one lapsed. Walter's contribution to the chronicling of events was now limited to his letters. From Clewer he wrote hurriedly to Agnes, enclosing a copy of his letter to his father and proposing to meet her in Hyde Park – 'I shall be in the Park on Tuesday if possible at 12.30 – 1 o'clock but ain't quite certain'. In the event it was Wednesday when they met. Agnes's anger of the previous week was forgotten, dissolved perhaps in her satisfaction that Walter was now pressing his father to act. Later that day, however, Walter sent Sir Thomas's reply and his own gloomy comment –

My own sweet child,

I did so enjoy seeing you today in the Park. I send you Sir Thomas's letter. It is, I fear, rather a hopeless one. You see by his account he must have overspent himself tremendously. He has, I find, mortgaged the estate £25,000 to pay his election expenses – £1000 a year clean gone. And then my eldest sister is the only one he has paid off, and has left all the rest chargeable on the property. He can't provide for me and leaves me to provide for my brothers and sisters after his death. If I'd only known he's played ducks and drakes with his money to such an extent that he couldn't provide for me when I wanted to marry, I'd have avoided you whenever I met you and so prevented myself from falling in love with you.

Don't show anyone Sir T's letter till I see you in the Park, and write me yards about what you think ought to be the next step. No, not whilst there is a gleam of hope will I give you up, you are too great a prize. But on the other hand I mustn't forget that, if every ray of hope is gone, it isn't fair on my part to see or write to you because, do you see, a woman must marry, a man needn't. If you don't marry me you must marry somebody else. Do you think it cruel of me, saying this? It's truth, alas.

Meanwhile he hoped to meet her at one or other of the fashionable balls that were being held almost every night at this time. Armed with the knowledge of which ones the Pitt-Rivers were likely to attend he left his visiting-cards with those hostesses who might invite him. As for Sir Thomas's letter, the advice Agnes gave after she had read it was to appeal to his better nature and seek to arouse some spirit of generosity in him. To Walter this seemed a hopeless strategy –

My own darling,

I quite agree with you about Sir Thomas's letters, but it's really perfectly useless writing sentiment to him. He only says 'bosh' and looks at everything in a mercenary manner. I would marry you tomorrow on £700 a year, and would live abroad in some cheap place – I told my father that, but he said 'I won't allow you to marry on £700 a year, and I'm certain the General won't allow his daughter to do so'. If I had £500 a year or had anything of my own I would just walk into church with you and marry you this very next week, and see one's parents to blazes. See? But I simply haven't got a brass farthing. We should have nothing in the world to live upon. I'm sure that the General would give you simply nothing if you made a runaway match of it.

Sir Thomas goes on the good father line and says he wouldn't be a friend to me if he allowed me to marry on a small income – and I honestly believe he thinks so. He thinks a man an egregious ass who marries for anything but money, and looks upon being in love with a woman like a slight cold in the head: a fortnight will cure it. And yr. father I consider just exactly as bad.

Do you understand me darling when I say the whole thing lies thus – Sir Thomas won't give me an income such as I asked him, and he also told me that he could not allow me more than £400 a year and the general says he certainly won't give you more than 300 a year, and my father says that unless yr. father gives more than 300 a year he won't even give 400. So you see I can't see anything more hopeless.

And then what you say about my going out and getting money. Money is a necessity, as you say, and every man can earn money if he chooses. But now if I wanted to earn money there are hardly anything to be procurable for a person in my position. I was never a clever boy at school, never took any trouble about learning anything, and now it's perfectly impossible for me to earn more than £100 a year as a clerk in an office, as all government offices are closed to me because I couldn't pass an examination for them.

The writer of that letter, it must be emphasised, was a thirty-year-old magistrate and heir to a baronetcy and a large estate. His pitiable incapacity was due to the caste and class system of his time, although the thought never seemed to occur to him. Instead he hoped, vaguely and with no real grounds for doing so. The factory inspectorship, recommended by Aunt Maude, was obviously beyond his grasp. Walter made some enquiries through a friend, but the subject was not mentioned again. The intervention of St. George seemed to languish for some inscrutable reason. And Agnes's entries in her journal became increasingly terse and staccato, as if she hardly trusted herself to do more than note the barest outline of each day. She jotted down the names of people she had met during the day, the initials R.I. when she had been to the Royal Institution, and not much else. The combination of subterfuge and disappointment put a pressure on her that inhibited her writing. There was one exception, however – a day in early May when her pent-up feelings overflowed into her journal –

> Got up rather late. On account of hearing a row going on when on the stairs, I refrained from going down further – therefore went without breakfast but it did not do much good. I was flown at at luncheon and bored to death almost, having already had it pretty severely from the minor one all the morning. I was told to write and tell you not to come to the ball, which I did, but I was in hopes you would, so I went.
>
> In the afternoon I was just going to the lecture when Mama, who had been hatching stories to Papa all the time, suddenly hit upon an unfortunate phrase of mine, 'The Man has no heart'. He tramped up and said 'You go to not a single place the whole of this season' about a dozen times, nothing else varied it. Occasionally 'You don't go out once this season, mind you' etc. etc.
>
> I am seldom amused at his rows but this *did* amuse me, and as he was tramping down again I was all trembling with the suddenness and unexpectedness of the whole thing. I tried to stammer out something about his being so good and kind on the contrary, when the sense of the ludicrous presented itself to me and I broke down in a hopeless giggle! It's about the only time I've not flown into a temper when he's been violent, and made matters ten times worse, but this did seem *so* ridiculous I couldn't be angry. So I made up!

The course of events in the fortnight following that outburst is not easy to follow. The General may well have been out of patience with Agnes, for he was now engaged – though he may not have told her so – in informal discussions with Walter's father and was finding him difficult to deal with. The immediate position was clear enough. Sir Thomas would give Walter an immediate allowance of £400 a year, and no more; the General would give Agnes £300. This was not regarded as a paticularly happy arrangement by any of those concerned, but of course it was only a short-term measure. The last of the elderly Grove aunts must die soon, to the financial advantage of Sir Thomas who could then treat Walter more handsomely. Beyond that were the consequences of the eventual deaths of the two fathers, particularly if in the meantime Sir Thomas married again.

In these circumstances it is easy to understand that the two men were greatly attracted to a policy of procrastination and were accordingly irritated by the impulsive headlong urgency of their children. Walter was normally docile enough for his father to restrain. Agnes was a different matter. At the risk of appearing 'unmaidenly' – as she put it – she was driving Walter on to some immediate action, while allowing her own parents no peace on the subject.

Her journal at this time is spare and uncommunicative. On Sundays she went to St. Peter's church, morning and evening, and sometimes to Sunday School. She notes the balls she attended – usually with the hope, one suspects, of finding Walter among the dancers. 'I expected you all the time. Cruel disappointment' is typical of such entries. The control on her correspondence was evidently tightened. On May 15 she wrote 'Came home, found my letter to Walter had been taken. Then began most trying fortnight of my existence. Got letter, did not send it of course. *I* hate my letters being read. Walter says he doesn't mind'. Two days later she comments 'Miserable day. My letters kept'. She apparently tried using Lionel instead of Alice as her means of communication, to judge from a sad note of Walter's which probably belongs to this period, though it bears no address or date –

> I was so disappointed today not meeting you. I called here after church and waited till 2 o'clock and then had to go out to lunch and Lionel's letter hadn't come then. I thought that you couldn't come out for some reason and couldn't let me know. I walked down to Tattersall's through the Park with Harry Pleydell on the off chance of seeing something of you and walked back again through the Park. Harry and I sat there for a long time till half past five. Oh my dear sweet child, the whole thing is so annoying.

Harry Pleydell was a personal friend of Walter's. The Mansel-Pleydells, to give them their full name, lived at Whatcombe in the

Winterborne valley southwest of Blandford. A prominent Dorset family, they were closely connected with the Mansels of Manston and the Clavells of Smedmore in the Isle of Purbeck. Harry's brother, Edmund, later married 'Kat' Grove – Walter's sister. The father of Harry and Edmund, John Clavell Mansel-Pleydell, was an authority on the natural history of Dorset: his scientific interests brought him into an intimate association and friendship with General Pitt-Rivers.

When Agnes noted in her journal on May 16 'Robert Smith's ball. Enjoyed very much. Danced good deal with Mr. Pleydell' it is easy to understand her pleasure. In the absence of Walter, his friend and confidante would be the best possible substitute and could answer reassuringly Agnes's enquiries for the latest news of her beloved.

The cheerful tone of this entry is a rare interlude in the sombre chronicle of May. Between the 8th and the 26th Walter was either absent from London or unable to make any personal contact with Agnes, due to the parental blockade. To make matters worse, Alice and Lionel were ill. As the days passed Agnes felt 'very dull and lonely and sad'. From Aunt Maude she heard that Lady Frances Osborne had said 'she had never seen anyone looking so unhappy as I was. No wonder everyone says I am looking ill and worn'. There seemed to be nobody to offer a word of sympathy, and she exclaimed 'It is misery and I only hope it may soon be all over'.

Chapter Eight

While the General and Sir Thomas were absorbed in their campaign of mutual attrition, St. George seems to have been trying to outflank them. One of the very few flashes of cheerfulness in Agnes's journal during May describes a walk she took with St. George, Lionel, Alice and Ursula's husband – Willy Scott – in the hope of meeting Walter. She had sent him a note, but he did not appear. However she talked to St. George 'and felt oh so hopeful, almost dazed with excitement and joy'. The cause of her excitement seems to be reflected in an undated letter from Walter, written from Salisbury on the notepaper of the Prince of Wales Own Royal Wiltshire Yeomanry, in which Walter served. He had had a letter from Mrs. Pitt-Rivers in formal terms requiring him to promise not to write to Agnes 'till all was settled'. Before replying he wanted to assure Agnes that it was simply 'a matter of time, before all would be well'. He continued –

> St. George is a perfect angel. He has offered me a secretaryship in his new company, £300 a year. Well, I have accepted it and I am waiting for a letter from him as to when he wants me to enter on my duties. I think of course I shall have to enter into those duties without being engaged to you formally, just to see if I can fulfill those duties which I feel certain I can fulfill. And then, joy – we shall be able to marry.

This was indeed a straw for Walter to clutch at. The figure of £300 suggests that St. George may have decided to offer himself as an alternative to the General as the provider of Agnes's dowry. The General's offer of the same amount was accompanied by conditions that Sir Thomas was refusing to accept. It seems likely that St. George's quixotic nature was aiming for an end to the legalistic wrangling between the two fathers.

Walter was predictably ready to lean on St. George. When Agnes tried to spur him on to fresh endeavours he replied 'Of course, darling child, I am going to speak to Sir Thomas but I shall wait till I hear from St. George. I'm sorry you ain't pleased with me, darling.' By the end of May he was relying heavily on St. George to intervene directly with Sir Thomas –

> I called on St. George and arranged an interview for Sir Thomas with St. George. What Sir Thomas says is this – 'What security have I that yr. secretaryship will be a permanence? The company may bust or never see the light, and it or you may be let in for a lot of money'.
>
> I have seen St. George about it and he is going to put it all right with Sir Thomas on that point. I have also written a rather strong letter to Sir Thomas that I think will have a good effect. I want to marry you the first week in July.
>
> I have been dining with St. George tonight. He is so nice and he is going to arrange everything with Sir Thomas. I think I shall go out of London as I hate the feeling of being so close to you and not seeing you, my sweet pet. I do want to speak to you so.

The meeting between St. George and Sir Thomas did not have the desired result. No more was heard of Walter's secretaryship. Good intentions were not enough. What Sir Thomas was looking for was the absolute security of a guaranteed annual payment of £300 for the rest of Agnes's life or a lump sum of £7500 which, invested at 4% would produce £300 p.a. That was the sort of language that Sir Thomas was using in his negotiations with the General; and in his turn the General was insisting that the Ferne estate must be secured beyond doubt for Walter and the children of the marriage. The prospect of a secretaryship in St. George's new company was too flimsy a fabric to build on.

So matters stood on what Agnes called 'a day of importance' – May 30, 1882. It began in a commonplace way with a French lesson and a visit to the Royal Institution to hear a lecture on Digestion. When she came home she found a letter from Sir Thomas and later there was one from Walter to Mrs. Pitt-Rivers. In her cryptic way at

Agnes Gerladine Fox-Pitt. The earliest extant portrait: a pencil sketch by an unknown artist

Above. Agnes's father, Colonel Augustus Henry Lane Fox, who became General Pitt-Rivers after his inheritance of the Pitt estates

Left. Agnes's sister, Alice, who married Sir John Lubbock (later Lord Avebury)

ʀushmore as it was when Agnes's father inherited it from Horace Pitt-Rivers, 6th Baron Rivers

'he dining-room at Rushmore during the lifetime of the last Lord Rivers (who died in 1880)

Kathleen Grove, Corinna Bruce, Charlotte Grove, Grace Bruce – the Committee of the Ferne Lawn Tennis Club, 1879. The Bruces were cousins of the Groves. A frond of fern was an appropriate emblem for the special outfit worn in the early years of lawn tennis

T.F. Grove, Mrs. Grove, Walter, Capt. Chaplin
Edith, Charlotte, Kathleen, Tom

A family group at Ferne in about 1869. Agnes's future husband, Walter Grove, is here an elegant Etonian with his mother and father, younger brother and sisters

Ferne House in 1850: the ancestral home of the Groves, built in 1811 to replace a much earlier house

A signpost still points the way to Ferne (now demolished) and Rushmore (now Sandroyd School)

Left. Sir Thomas Fraser Grove M.P. Gladstone rewarded him for his political services with a baronetcy in 1874

Right. Frances, second wife of Sir Thomas Grove: known familiarly as 'Grovina'

A portrait of Agnes by Max Bohm

this period Agnes commented 'Unsatisfactory at first' but then she continued –

> Soon St. George came in and put quite a different face on matters. Papa stealthy – says he could not do any more for us. Long discussions with the rest of the family. All thought of course that Papa ought to give more. But if he won't what's to be done? St. George offers to satisfy Sir Thomas on the question of settlements, but is it right to accept it? I don't mind, and no one could, the way he does it. He says it might look ostentatious but he has the most generous kind heart and noble charitable disposition in existence, I am sure, and I simply think he is an angel brought down to benefit mankind! If only tomorrow would settle all. I'm simply ill.

What St. George now proposed was, quite simply, to come up with £7500 on the wedding day as Agnes's dowry. The General was not pleased – either because he doubted St. George's ability to produce such a sum, or because the unconditional offer weakened his strategy in dealing with Sir Thomas.

Before she finally went to bed after that momentous family conference Agnes was called downstairs to hear from her mother that Walter had been told to call next morning at eleven o'clock. After which Agnes 'slept in peace and joy'. Walter duly presented himself and two hours later Sir Thomas arrived. 'He did not talk nicely', Agnes commented, 'I was furious with all he said'. She spent a miserable afternoon, crying her eyes out, until St. George came and reproved her. One by one the other members of the family came in, but still there was no news. At length Alice brought Agnes the good news that such progress was being made that Walter had been invited to call again the following morning. She closed her journal that night with a flourish – 'I bounded upstairs a different person'.

Next morning the family all went to the Trooping of the Colour, leaving Agnes to muse on the anxious days of the previous month. 'I have felt so powerless and so misunderstood by all but Walter', she wrote, 'and he has been so seldom with me. I think even *he* little knows how much I really love him. Even I did not, till a little while ago. Now I have realised the fact that I cannot live without him'.

Soon after the family's return Walter arrived and had an interview with the General, of which the outcome was – in Agnes's words – 'chaos and darkness in my heart'. Her father came up to her room and said 'It's no use, Sir Thomas refuses his consent – so there's an end of it.' Agnes's reception of this news hardly needs describing. 'I rushed away, couldn't answer' are her own words. And the General? Was it pity for his daughter's distress that sent him out of the house, in search of Sir Thomas? As for the rest of the family, they felt the need for fresh air and took an afternoon stroll. Agnes was left to her own devices.

In the early evening the family began to reassemble. Mrs. Pitt-Rivers, Alice and Lionel were there and so too was Ursula, now pregnant and near her time. Papa appeared, and so did Walter. And in some unaccountably miraculous way the whole issue was settled and the wedding fixed for July 20. Looking now at the page in her journal, the ink a century old but plain enough, it is easy to share the feelings concentrated in the simplicity of 'Hurrah Hurrah'. For one young woman in Belgravia it was indeed a Glorious First of June.

What had passed between the General and Sir Thomas Grove is soon revealed. Both men left London immediately, the General returning to Rushmore. It had been expected that Sir Thomas would give formal expression to his consent in a letter before he left, but he had not done so. Walter was instructed to write to him. On June 4 General Pitt-Rivers received a letter from the Royal Dorset Yacht Club –

> My dear General,
>
> I hear from my son that you wish to know if I am satisfied with the arrangements made in the event of his marrying yr. daughter. So I write to say that the arrangements proposed as I understand them viz that you give £300 a year during yr. life and that £7500 is to be settled by you to be paid to my son after yr. death subject to the provisions of the marriage settlement and that I allow £400 a year and a hundred more when the annuity to my aunt falls in, are satisfactory to me.
>
> I am willing to settle the Ferne estate on my son. In fact I have already done so, by will.
>
> Yrs very truly
> Thos. F. Grove.

In London meanwhile Walter had taken rooms at 10 Ebury Street so that he could be near Grosvenor Gardens and see Agnes every day. 'Mama is very nice to him', she noted, 'and I am sure likes him very

very much'. Her engagement to Walter was tacitly acknowledged and phrases like 'Blessed heavenly day' and 'Blissfully happy afternoon' began to appear in her journal.

There were two events, however, which clouded her happiness. One was the death of Ursula's baby within two hours of its birth. The other, a few days later, was the departure of Lionel to Canada. 'Feel parting with the dear boy very much', she wrote, 'we have been such friends'. It is certainly the case that the references to Lionel in her journal have a special tone of affection, even when she is criticising him. At Rushmore in the previous winter she recorded how they hunted together, played billiards and planned dances and parties, and Lionel flirted with the local girls, with Kat Grove and Grace Farquharson – sometimes to Agnes's annoyance. 'I hate to hear Lionel speak about women', she wrote, 'He says "They're only meant to amuse men", and drawls'. But her attitude becomes endearingly solicitous when his cynical defences are pierced – 'Lionel is, I am afraid, badly in love. I wish he weren't but will do my best for him'. Alas, only ten days were to pass before Lionel left the country. There is no knowing if unrequited love drove him to this action but he spent several years in Canada.

For the rest of June there were no clouds in Agnes's sky. Walter was in close attendance, Mama was benign, there were agreeable visits to dressmakers and jewellers, and welcoming smiles at 40 Dover Street when Grandmama Stanley and Aunt Maude received a visit from the young couple. The entries in the journal became perfunctory as if life were now too good to need any comment. The one exception was a brief lovers' tiff which suddenly animated Agnes's very feminine sensibility –

> Coming home had a quarrel with W. I never in my life cared so much about anyone speaking to me – only I couldn't own myself wrong after. I did at first, but he went on, and even now I expect I shall pretend I'm not.
>
> And I never felt so angry with myself before, for caring.

To make matters worse he had given her, that very morning – 'a lovely present, a fly-pin'. Happily the sudden flash of temper was quickly forgotten and they were soon riding in the Park or eating bananas and strawberries with Harry Pleydell in a railway train during a visit to Windsor. The progress of the marriage settlement went unmentioned. The lawyers were now dealing with that and had no occasion to disturb Agnes's peace of mind.

This is not to say, however, that Frederick W. Farrer of 66 Lincoln's Inn Fields was enjoying his correspondence with Sir Thomas Grove. It began equably enough on June 14 when he wrote to acknowledge a letter from Sir Thomas suggesting a meeting to prepare the marriage settlement. In his reply Mr. Farrer explained that, though General Pitt-Rivers had told him about the proposed marriage, the General had not given him definite instructions. He would therefore see the General promptly and write again, which he did. With commendable speed he despatched the General's proposals within two days and proposed an appointment with Sir Thomas to discuss practical questions about the Ferne estate in financial detail.

Sir Thomas did not like the General's proposals. There was a suggestion that the extra £100 Sir Thomas was to pay when his aunt's annuity ended would be offset by a reduction of £100 in the General's allowance to Agnes – so that the only person to benefit from the aunt's death would be the General. There was also a proposal that the conversion of Agnes's annual allowance into a lump sum of £7500 capital should not take place until after the death of not only the General but also his wife. Aware of St. George's intervention Sir Thomas countered with a readiness to accept the immediate capital amount from the General's son.

Mr. Farrer dutifully referred this to the General with a request for further instructions. Fortified with these he informed Sir Thomas that he had seen the General on the subject and 'he wishes me to say that he will have nothing to do with it if his son, St. George, is to pay £7500 for his sister'. Having conveyed this uncompromising message Mr. Farrer thought it prudent to add 'Looking to all the circumstances of the case I think it hardly possible that I should act for you as well as for General Pitt-Rivers, and I must ask you to get some other Solicitor to act on your behalf'.

Two days later all difficulties appeared to be overcome. Farrer wrote to Sir Thomas on June 22 – 'I have heard from General Pitt-Rivers that matters are accommodated between you and him, and that the Settlement is to be prepared on the basis of the letter I wrote you.' He again urged Sir Thomas to instruct another solicitor; pressed him for a certified rental of the Ferne Estate and other financial information; and warned him that 'it will be impossible for the marriage to take place by the 20th of next month unless every exertion is made.'

Six days later Farrer was still pressing the same subjects. He then received a letter from Sir Thomas which varied so much from the terms thought to be agreed that, in exasperation, he forwarded it to the General and asked for further instructions. What was at issue now was the security of Walter's inheritance. Here Mrs. Pitt-Rivers intervened and told Walter to write to his father immediately and reason with him. Obediently Walter did so –

27th June. 10 Ebury Street.

My Dear Sir T,

Mrs. Rivers asked me to write to you. The General says that of course he can't trust to yr. will as it is simply no settlement, and as for the reason you give that the Ferne property you don't wish alienated – of course if it was entailed on my son it couldn't possibly be so. He says he will be satisfied with the Ferne estate only being entailed as I have told him it's a great thing for you to have the power to sell or exchange Winterslow. He thinks you had better come up to London and bring all the requisite deeds to Farrer or the settlements will never be finished in time. I don't see what objection you can have to entailing the Ferne property on me as you are never likely to want to sell any of it, as you have no outlying bits and it is so compact already. Do please hurry up or nothing will be done, as we are no more forward than we were 10 days ago.

Yrs. Walter Grove.

And so it went on. Farrer patiently restated what the General now considered to be agreed proposals. Stubbornly Sir Thomas continued to insist that he did not intend to tie up his Ferne estate – 'nor is it reasonable to expect me to do so'. Having despatched this defiant note on June 30 he departed over the weekend to 11 Gloucester Row, Weymouth – his home during the yachting season. His motive is easy to understand: his will was something he could amend later if he wished, but an entail was a different matter.

Farrer now reminded him that 'Mr. Grove is your eldest son and on the occasion of his marriage a considerable and certain inheritance ought to be secured to him on your death'. He returned to the point on July 7 explaining that the General, whose attitude he considered 'perfectly reasonable', wanted simply to be certain 'that your eldest son (and his eldest son if he has one) shall at your death be in the position that an eldest son ought to be'.

The burden of Sir Thomas's complaint was that he would be reduced to the position of an 'annuitant' on his own property. He sent a long rambling letter of righteous expostulation to Mrs. Pitt-Rivers, protesting that when his daughters had married 'men of property' he did not try to force *them* to entail their estates. With the wedding only a fortnight away, ominous signs began to appear in Agnes's journal that the negotistions might break down at any moment. She referred to 'an objectionable letter from Sir T.' Next day Walter went to Lincoln's Inn Fields to see Farrer, and on July 9 the bombshell burst. In Agnes's words – 'Papa talked to Walter, and he is not to be allowed to come here again till all is settled'.

Sir Thomas had sent Farrer an ultimatum. To avoid the entail he was prepared to accept an alternative arrangement which guaranteed Walter a fixed capital sum in cash or land when his father died. To avoid a further loss of time, spent in disputing the amount of this sum, the General was ready to make a swift compromise. On July 11 Farrer sent Sir Thomas a placatory letter signifying the General's acceptance of 'virtually the arrangement as you propose it'. Walter was readmitted to the Pitt-Rivers household and Agnes's life became so hectic that she temporarily halted the entries in her journal on July 10. Some weeks were to pass before she managed to search her memory for the material to set against July 11. Finally this is what she wrote –

> 11th Tuesday. I have left off here more than 3 weeks ago, and now I am a settled-down married woman. It does seem odd. I must try and remember what we did.
> Today is August 1st.

Chapter Nine

The wedding took place at St. Peter's, Eaton Square and was duly reported under the heading 'Court and Fashion'. The guests included a couple of Earls with their Countesses – Russell and Eldon – and various peers, representatives of noble families and prominent figures in London Society: there were Digbys and Glyns, Stanleys and Wimbornes, Conyers, Thynnes, du Boulays and Bartle Freres, in impressive numbers. Agnes had half a dozen bridesmaids – her own sister, Alice; Walter's two sisters, Charlotte and Kate; and three cousins. Walter's best man was Harry Pleydell. The ceremony was conducted jointly by Canon Wilkinson of St. Peter's and Horace Chapman of Donhead St. Andrew. Agnes regularly attended St. Peter's when she was in London and had a high regard for Mr. Wilkinson. The choice of Horace Chapman recognised the situation of Ferne in his parish of Donhead St. Andrew. He was moreover no obscure and humble country parson but a man of solid social connections: subsequently one of his daughters married the future Viscount Allenby while another married Admiral Napier.

Behind the pomp and circumstance we can catch a glimpse or two of the excitement and the nervousness that Agnes recorded in her journal –

> July 20th. Thursday. *My wedding day!* Today a great step in my life. The great step of one's whole life. I got up very early and went to church and met Aunt Maud; and then after breakfast I went out again and saw Mr. Wilkinson. He talked to me and I am sure helped me a good deal. He gave me several books.

> Then the usual thing – I dressed and at half past eleven was in church and married. We signed everything and came home to breakfast. Then I talked and laughed and felt very gay, and so was Walter after it was all over, but before he was dreadfully nervous. And then we went off in the carriage and Harry Pleydell had gone before with Walter's luggage and Tawny.

Tawny was a pet dog which accompanied them to Clewer Manor where they spent the first days of their married life as the guests of Walter's sister, Edith and her husband, Edmund Benson Foster. Clewer is close to Windsor so Agnes and Walter were able to visit St. George's Chapel, where they got very good seats and admired the singing. They also went on the Thames and were towed along. Agnes noted that 'Someone saw us under one umbrella! It was lovely'. In the main their days at Clewer were relaxed and uneventful – 'blissful peaceful days, so quiet and happy'.

After a week they moved on to Brighton and livelier company. They went to Goodwood Races, watched the polo in Preston Park and played cards at night for something more than the sixpence Agnes used to win from Lionel at billiards. Their principal companions were the Benett Stanfords, a wealthy couple whose country seat was Pyt House between Tisbury and Semley, and only half a dozen miles from Ferne. Stanford had started life as Vere Fane and then followed the Victorian custom of adding the names from which he drew his prestige and his wealth. His mother was the heiress of the Benetts, a prominent family in the Shaftesbury area. In Charles I's reign a Colonel Benett had represented Shaftesbury in Parliament and was probably the Thomas Benett of Pyt House who married Margaret Grove of Ferne in 1623. Benetts and Groves in succeeding generations were politically active. On the stone frontage of the Boot Inn in Tisbury you may still see the large and handsomely carved slogan *Benett and Independence*, dating from the campaigning of John Benett who was first elected to Parliament in 1819.

Having adopted his maternal grandfather's name Vere Fane Benett then married Ellen Stanford, who was reputed to own half Brighton – a good reason for making sure that the name of Stanford did not perish. Thus did Colonel Vere Fane Benett Stanford blossom in his ultimate splendour; and lest he should seem to be lacking in filial piety he installed in Semley church a memorial window to his parents, Arthur and Lucy Fane.

Although they were somewhat older than Walter and Agnes the Benett Stanfords became close friends and Agnes's later diaries contain many references to Pyt House. At Brighton the card playing circle included Lord and Lady Parker, and the stakes evidently impressed Agnes as she noted the size of her winnings one night – two pounds and ten shillings. From Brighton she and Walter took a trip by boat on August 3rd down the Channel to Plymouth, and thence by rail to Penzance. At Lands End they found 'such quantities of tourists'. They left their travelling maid, Elizabeth, at Penzance while they sailed to the Scillies but when Mr. Dorrien Smith invited them to stay on the island of Tresco they sent instructions to Elizabeth to bring more of their luggage. Meanwhile they amused themselves catching sparrows with the eldest of the four Dorrien Smith children, Arthur.

From Tresco they journeyed to Malmesbury to stay with Walter's friends, the Trafalgars; and finally to Ferne after a brief stop in London. They had been away for about a month. For the rest of the summer they followed no particular plan, taking each day as it came, visiting their friends in the neighbourhood of Ferne and Rushmore and enjoying the familiar pleasures of country life. They went to a cricket match at Pyt House and a rabbit shoot on Win Green. On another visit to Pyt House Agnes beat Walter at billiards before going out for a drive in Mrs. Benett Stanford's chay. They saw Fonthill Towers and Agnes commented 'lovely drive, pleasantest company in England'.

Another agreeable drive was from Ferne through Tollard Royal, over Thickthorn Down and along the Tarrant valley to Kingston Lacy, the home of the Bankes family. Surely no house in England has a finer approach than the mile-long avenue of beeches running past Badbury Rings to the lodge that leads into Kingston Lacy park. This, like Pyt House, was one of the friendly and hospitable houses which Walter and Agnes frequently visited. On this occasion the houseparty drove down to Bournemouth on one day to see Edward Farquharson win the lawn tennis championship.

Like his father, 'Squire' Farquharson, Edward was a vivid and lively character. A natural athlete he once challenged a professional fighter in a boxing booth at Woodbury Hill Fair. Cheered on by some farmer friends who had wagered on him Farquharson knocked out the 'Champion' who complained that he wasn't looking! The proprietor refused to pay the stake money and the free-for-all that followed made local history. The Bere Regis police were unable to cope and had to send to Dorchester for reinforcements.

When they left Kingston Lacy Agnes and Walter drove to Tarrant Gunville, to have lunch at Eastbury with Ed Farquharson's brothers Henry and Richard. The surviving part of Eastbury House was not used as a residence until some time after 1867, having served for many years as Squire Farquharson's kennels and hunt headquarters. His son, Richard, had now brought it back into use as a family residence. Like his brother Ed, Richard Farquharson was a spirited character – red-haired and quick tempered. He stood for Parliament solely, as he explained, from his hatred of the Whig, Portman of Bryanston, with whom he had had a hunting quarrel. He libelled his opponent, lost the election, but beat him at the second attempt.

By mid-September Agnes and Walter were back at Ferne. Sir Thomas was not at home. On the 21st they received news that he had married, two days previously. The new Lady Grove was Frances Hinton Best, a daughter of Henry Northcote of Crediton. She had been twice widowed. Her first husband was Captain Crosse, her second Captain Hon. Frederick Barnewall Best, the second son of Lord Wynford. The Wynfords lived at Charlton House, barely a couple of miles from Ferne, and had a town house in Grosvenor Gardens so Sir Thomas's bride was no stranger to her new circumstances. Some time elapsed before she met Walter and Agnes because they left Ferne almost immediately, going first to Clewer for a few days and then to Montacute, the home of the Phelips family. They were planning to visit the United States and Willy Phelips had decided to go with them. There were brief farewell visits to Rushmore and Ferne before they set off to Liverpool, where Aunt Maude was waiting at the station to wish them a safe crossing. Agnes bought a rug with the £10 the General had given her, and on October 21st she, Walter and Willy Phelips boarded the s.s. *Servia*, bound via Queenstown for New York.

They had a rough crossing. During the first five days most of the passengers were very ill, but conditions then improved. Agnes spent much of her time reading Browning, Byron and Anstey's *Vice Versa*, which had just been published. Her shipboard acquaintances included Lord Tarbat, Dr. McKellar and a New York hostess, Mrs. Thurber. When the *Servia* arrived in New York a band played to greet Adelina Patti, who was one of the passengers.

Agnes's first impression of the city was 'Bad Streets, noisy and dirty' and she disliked the rooms they had engaged. Eventually they moved to the Westminster Hotel which had 'shocking bad food' but could offer 'lovely rooms'. The new friendship with Mrs. Thurber blossomed quickly. They dined together and went to hear the opera, *L'Africaine*. American hospitality was freely offered and Agnes's diary records a weekend spent away from New York city, which involved a railway journey and a night drive with a black coachman to what she describes as a 'nice wooden house'. Next day their hosts, the Hewitts, drove them through the countryside of high hills and wild rocky scenery. They had tea in a log-cabin belonging to the youngest Miss Hewitt and next day they returned to New York where the hospitable Hewitts provided seats for them at the opera house to hear Patti in *Faust*.

They now settled into a fresh hotel, the Buckingham, and enjoyed the varied entertainment and the social life that New York could offer. They went to the Christie Minstrels, lunched and dined at Delmonico's, visited friends and met Oscar Wilde at a party given by Mrs. Botta where a sculptor named Story read some of his poems. Another day the Thurbers took Agnes and Walter to see the Fire Brigade and afterwards to an oyster supper at Dorlan's. Unfortunately Agnes caught a chill and became 'very ill with coughing' in spite of having bought what she calls 'a chest preserver'. A homoeopathic doctor attended her and advised a change of air.

Accordingly she and Walter set out on 24 November, accompanied by Willy Phelips, to visit Niagara. They went first to Prospect House on the Canadian side of the Falls, having their first impression of the spectacle by moonlight. They telegraphed Lionel to meet them later: Agnes would be eager to know how he had fared in Canada since his arrival there in June. Meanwhile she enjoyed a couple of days exploring the Falls. Her journal describes how they 'went to table rock underneath the falls – all dressed up in oilskins etc., spray very violent but quite wonderful. Went on to burning spring. Whirlpool rapids.' Next day –

> Drove again first to Park Island. To see the falls quite close from above – these are the American falls and one crosses over the bridge for which one has to pay enormous sums, and then down by the tramway to see the Falls from below. Both equally marvellous and beautiful, and then we went to Goat

> Island. I got a Canadian fox's head the other side. We went round everything and saw everything, and one thing delighted us more than another as we went on.

Their next stop after Niagara was Cleveland. Agnes admired its 'nice quaint houses' and thought it one of the prettiest cities she had seen. Euclid Avenue in particular was 'quite lovely'. After a heavy snowfall the tall electric light illuminated the snow on the trees and in the square outside the hotel in a way that delighted her.

At Cleveland they parted from Willy Phelips, who returned to New York. Agnes and Walter planned to meet Lionel in Chicago, breaking their journey for a night at Toledo. They did not retain happy memories of Toledo which Agnes thought a dirty uninteresting city; and although she had no complaints about her room at Boody's Hotel her maid Elizabeth found bugs in hers. Chicago, by contrast, impressed Agnes as a wonderful place 'when one thinks that less than ten years ago it was nothing, and was burnt down five years ago.'

The reunion with her brother was not as she had anticipated. She found him much changed.

> After breakfast we were downstairs when a person with a beard came up and shook hands with us – who turned out to be Lionel. We went upstairs and talked, and then went out for a walk. I do not know what to make of Lionel: he seemed to talk very sensibly and well, and we thought he had been hardly treated, but since then something has happened to make me suspicious.'

What that 'something' was remained hidden until a week later when Agnes and Walter were back in New York. Lionel telegraphed an urgent request to Walter for a hundred dollars, which seemed odd to Agnes because, as she wrote in her journal –

> We know he had £100 in his possession, but Walter sent it to him. Yesterday a letter came from him to Walter, and Walter won't tell me about it – not even yes or no – and Lionel at the end said 'Don't tell anyone, not even Agnes'. I wonder what it can be?. When I ask Walter if he had done anything wrong he doesn't answer.
>
> I have since found out that Lionel lost his money to a horrid man who took him to his house and made him gamble it all

> away after having stood him several drinks at the bar. Walter told me because he thought I might say something rash about it at home. Of course I do not intend to mention it.

With this unhappy episode concluded Agnes settled down to enjoy a month of socializing in New York. There were parties for luncheon and dinner, and in between she called on her new friends and acquaintances in the customary fashion of the period – sometimes recording whether they were 'in' or 'out'. Her journal is replete with their names. There were the Vanderbilts and Lady Mandeville and others who may perhaps have more significance today for American readers than for British – the Hewitts, the Mariés, Miss Coddington, Mrs. Thurber, the Livingstons and Pelham Clinton. No doubt they figured in the social news and gossip of the time, even though the aura of celebrity has faded from them.

There were several visits to the theatre: in ten days before Christmas Walter and Agnes went to the Madison Square Theatre to see 'Young Mr. Winthrop', to an unnamed theatre to see 'The Sorcerer', to a production of 'Twelfth Night' at Booth's Theatre, and to 'a theatre down East' with the Thurbers. And there were the balls at Delmonico's. At the first she attended Agnes noted the presence of several Englishmen. At the next, four nights later, she was requested by McAllister to lead the cotillon. This was presumably a great compliment. Ward McAllister has been described as the 'ringmaster' of New York's wealthy and fashionable circle. He could hardly fail to notice a young and beautiful visitor from the English aristocracy: before the first ball of the new year he sent her a bouquet.

In the midst of these activities Agnes decided to learn the banjo. This instrument was presumably the craze of the period, as the mandoline had been earlier and the guitar became in our own time. What started Agnes was the gift of a banjo as a Christmas present from Mrs. Thurber. She and Walter had several invitations to spend some part of Christmas Day with their New York friends and it proved to be what Agnes called 'a very joyous day for me'.

> We went to church, and Walter and I stayed together for the Communion. I felt so extremely happy – it joined us together more than ever. Then we lunched with Miss Butler. She gave me a book of Aldrich's poems, and he Emerson's essays. In afternoon we went to tea with the Mariés. In evening we dined

> with Thurbers. Miss Wheller and Liz there. Mrs. Thurber gave me a banjo and he a croqodile and some shells.

The mind boggles at what the 'croqodile' may have been, but there is no mistaking the banjo. The very next day Agnes called on 'the banjo man' and arranged for lessons to begin at once. Over the next few days there are repeated references to visits from 'banjo master' or 'banjo man', followed later by 'practised banjo' and a final triumphant 'played banjo'.

In the first days of January they went to Brooklyn, where they lunched at 'a little inn'; and they also visited the Vanderbilt mansion which Agnes thought 'very fine, but gaudy and bad taste'. There were several heavy falls of snow and sleighriding became the new pleasure. After a weekend vist to Albany it was time to pack, to enjoy a last ball at Delmonico's, a final dinner with the Thurbers, and go aboard the s.s. *Paronia* bound for Liverpool.

The Atlantic in January is seldom benign. The knowledge that she was nearly seven months pregnant must have made Agnes the more apprehensive but she endured her discomfort stoically. The ocean was very rough, and she was very ill, but she noted gratefully that her stewardess was 'a charming person' who took great care of her.

It was raining and cold when she and Walter arrived at Liverpool at midday on 27 January 1883. Five hours later a tug put them ashore and they arrived at 4 Grosvenor Gardens at midnight. Mama was waiting up to receive them.

Chapter Ten

The return from America marked the end of the honeymoon. Walter and Agnes picked up the threads of everyday life at Ferne while they planned how to deal with Agnes's impending confinement. Walter made several journeys to London to look at houses, presumably because Agnes wanted to be near her London doctor, McClagan. It was eventually decided to rent a furnished place for the confinement. For a permanent home they had the prospective use of a farmhouse – Easton Farm – at Berwick St. John. To put the place in proper order for their occupation Sir Thomas provided £300. Meanwhile they passed the months of February and March at Ferne. Agnes's personal maid, Elizabeth, who had made the American tour with them, now left to become the bride of Sergeant Ash – much missed by Agnes.

While Walter went hunting and shooting, Agnes remained inactive at Ferne with little to enter in her journal. Mrs. Benett Stanford called in the chay to take her for a drive to Pyt House, and there was a brief visit from Lionel for what Agnes described as 'another edition of his love story' with Kathleen Grove. Almost at once he set off again for Canada, taking with him Tom Grove – Walter's younger brother.

There is virtually no reference at this time to Sir Thomas Grove's new wife, Frances. Back in September Walter and Agnes had left Ferne within twenty-four hours of hearing of the wedding and had subsequently gone to America without meeting Lady Grove. Whatever impression Agnes now formed, when they were perforce under the same roof at Ferne, was not confided to her journal. A connection between the event and Sir Thomas's readiness to settle Agnes and Walter in a home of their own at Berwick St. John is, however, easy to recognise.

The reserve between the two women was broken dramatically at the end of March. Sir Thomas was away from home. At Ferne Agnes decided to go over to Rushmore for luncheon, and Lady Grove accompanied her. They returned together at about four o'clock.

> The roads were very rough and jolted me a good deal. That afternoon providentially Fran and I became great friends. She insisted again upon me calling her Frances, and kissed me. At five I went down to tea after having conversed with Ella on my drawing, which I was painting in the schoolroom. I did not go up again until 7.30, having talked to Grovina all that time. After I had laid down a little, Walter came home. I did not go down to dinner as I felt rather uneasy. Time went on and it grew worse. At half past two on Friday morning March 30 my baby was born. I was quite alone and it came in about five minutes. I was very well. Mrs. Wright came up and delivered the child, and soon after the doctor came. Poor Walter was then happier, but during the time he was fetching Jane the baby came and no-one knew. Kind Frances sat up nearly all night with me.

From that context it is clear that 'Grovina' was the nickname Agnes and Walter had applied to Frances, Lady Grove – who now became 'kind Frances'. The baby, a girl, was christened 'Honor', though she also soon acquired a nickname – 'Dod' or 'Dode'.

Agnes contracted measles shortly after the birth and her health continued to be uncertain during the following months. Nevertheless she was eager to accompany Walter on a busy round of social engagements – London theatres and balls, Ascot races, a holiday in the Isle of Wight where she went canoeing, a day at the Eton-Winchester cricket match, and the ceaseless activity of shopping forays and formal calls on friends, neighbours and relatives in London. All this appealed to Agnes. The comparative solitude of her new home at Berwick St. John had a depressing effect on her when Walter was away. In a big house like Rushmore or Ferne there was usually company of a kind and the bustle of people coming and going. Easton farmhouse could be an excessively quiet and lonely place for someone as high-spirited as Agnes.

> July 19. I do dislike being alone all day. I have no horse or anything, a wretched cook, no food hardly, no one to see. My baby asleep, and when awake I am too busy to do anything. I am getting the house much more straight..
>
> I heard from my dear boy. Oh how I do miss him – no one knows. Tommorrow is our first wedding day.

It was a strange ending to a year so full of incident. However, Walter returned the following afternoon and the business of home-making soon began to yield a sense of satisfaction. Agnes had always taken a pride in her personal surroundings and she now became preoccupied with papering walls and putting up a dado. Parties from Rushmore and Ferne came to admire the domestic improvements and, as the summer unfolded, there was a constant traffic between the three houses. Imperceptibly Easton House, Berwick St. John, became an establishment in its own right as Walter and Agnes developed the texture of their married life and their own circle of friends.

Some of the names carefully chronicled in her record of visits made and received are already familiar – Harry Pleydell at Whatcombe, Willy Phelips at Montacute, the Farquharsons at Tarrant Gunville , the Benett Stanfords at Pyt House. Less familiar are lords Wolverton and Alington. Wolverton was George Grenfell Glyn, the second Baron Wolverton, a keen supporter of Gladstone and of hunting – two enthusiasms that he shared with the Groves. He owned a large estate in and around Iwerne Minister. Lord Alington had started life as Henry Gerard Sturt, heir to the great house and estate at Crichel. He became Baron Alington in 1876, after representing the county of Dorset in Parliament for twenty years without a break. He was certainly a useful friend to have: on one occasion he ordered a through train to stop at Tisbury so that Agnes could board it and travel with him.

Lord Wolverton's hunting headquarters at Iwerne were the setting for a curious incident that Agnes recorded in November 1883. She was invited to a day's hunting and borrowed a horse from her sister, Alice. Before she set out she noted in her journal 'a sort of presentiment of evil' which had kept her awake all night. She added the words 'Hope nothing will happen to me for the sake of my beloveds. My dear dear treasures'. A subsequent entry, written in different ink, recounts what happened.

> We got to the meet and my horse was waiting for me. I jumped the first fence, then I had a stupid fall – the first I have ever had. I got hung up by my stirrup but I got on alright again and joined them afterwards. We walked home quietly.

The year ended uneventfully, apart from a 'loathsome scandal' which was circulating about Mrs. Benett Stanford and her groom. Agnes sympathised with her friend's distress and tried to comfort her during a visit to Pyt House on Christmas Eve. The following afternoon there was a great gathering at Rushmore, though without the General who had gone to London – in search of peace, perhaps. The festivities lasted for three days, during which Agnes and the rest of the party 'played romps, danced about and had great fun.'

The words recall, not the previous Christmas in New York, but the one before – when Agnes and Walter were first attracted to each other, and Boxing Day provided the initial entry in the closely packed journal with the brass lock that she was now about to close. As she reached the final page Agnes seemed to recapture her original mood of moral endeavour and self-improvement.

> December 31st. Last day of this year, I finish this dear old book. Harry Pleydell left about 11, then I went for a walk to the top of the hill. I have settled to go for a walk every day, there is nothing so good for one. Then I painted before luncheon and after till dark. Then I wrote my letters till post. Now I intend to read, so altogether I consider this a very profitable day and hope all in the coming year may be as good. Amen.

In one respect the coming year brought a marked change. The dreamy passionate teenager was turning into the practical and self-assured wife and mother. Turning the pages from 1884 to 1887 one notices the growing emphasis on outward events, the witholding of her more intimate moods. The diary tends to become a habit, an engagement book, a hurried scribble, even a nuisance that she neglects. There are occasional gaps that cannot be filled, but it is still possible to recapture much of her daily life.

Her social life centred largely on Ferne and Rushmore with their constantly changing houseparties. There were also the big social occasions of the winter, such as the Blandford Ball and the Hunt Ball at Dorchester, and at an informal level the visits of two or three days at a time to their more intimate friends in the splendours of

Montacute and Whatcombe and Kingston Lacy. In summer there were village cricket matches and picnics in the Larmer Tree Gardens. It was a narrow world, albeit a very agreeable one. Excursions from it were to Weymouth for Yeomanry Week, when Walter looked glamorous and handsome in his uniform; to London for a bout of theatre-going and fashionable parties; or to Walter's sister at Clewer, where Agnes's honeymoon had started and which was so convenient for Ascot Races.

As might be expected with any young mother, Agnes was greatly preoccupied with family matters, with topics of marriage and parenthood among her nearest contemporaries. In 1884 the sad memory of her sister Ursula's stillborn child gave way to the good news of a daughter safely delivered. Her other sister, Alice, found her much desired escape from parental 'tyranny' in a marriage with one of her father's scientific colleagues, Sir John Lubbock; and she too was blessed, most expeditiously, with a daughter. Brother Lionel made another of his brief homecomings from Canada and took their younger brother, Douglas, back with him. The days of Lionel's romantic flirtations with Kate Grove were ending. A year after his departure she married Harry Pleydell's brother, Edmund, in a wedding which was first postponed and then overshadowed tragically by Harry's fatal illness. Harry had been Walter's staunchest friend, and Agnes had learnt to trust and confide in him during the difficult months before her marriage. His death was a severe blow.

In lighter vein Agnes's journal exhibits the versatility that must have been an attractive element in her personality. In the spring at Berwick St. John she was very much the kind of wife one might expect Walter Grove to have – a lively rider to hounds, picking herself up when the horse 'went head over heels' and noting 'Killed two foxes, I got one brush'. And then in June, at her grandmother Stanley's dinner table in London, taking her part in the Dover Street table-talk with Aunt Rosalind and Aunt Maude and some gentlemen of literary and artistic distinction – Sir Edward Poynter, Sir George Dasent, Tom Hughes the author of *Tom Brown's Schooldays*, and Bret Harte who at that time was U.S. Consul in Glasgow. It was a foretaste of things to come.

In the early years of her marriage it was the other element in her Stanley background – the hustings rather than the salon – that Agnes could fruitfully express in her marriage. Ferne was a Liberal stronghold. Sir Thomas had sat as Member for South Wiltshire from 1865 to 1874, when he was defeated by 900 votes. In 1885 he contested the Wilton Division and the excitement of polling day is reflected in Agnes's journal –

> December 1st. Charlotte came down, and she and Walt drove to the different polling places. I drove to Woodcuts to try and get King to vote but he would not. Walt dined at Ferne after having been to Charlton where there was a row and Mr. King's butler was beaten.
>
> December 2nd. Walter went off at 7 to Wilton. At 1.30 I got a telegram saying Sir T. had got in with a majority of 32. We went up to Ferne – greatest excitement. Sir T. and Walt made speeches outside the house. The band played, and there was beer and dancing.

The fact that the result brought no joy to General Pitt-Rivers may have appealed to the rebel in Agnes. Her father was a sort of aberrant Tory who refused to give a personal neighbourly support to Sir Thomas because he was both a Liberal (which was endurable) and a Radical (which was not); and Sir Thomas declined to disown the Radical cause. The General's anti-Radical sentiments took a more disagreeable form when one of his sons – unnamed, but it must have been St. George – became a vice-president of a Radical association. On the General's instructions Mr. Creech, his land steward, 'made it know that your son has no connection with you' and promised to get a paragraph to this effect in the county papers. Agnes's sympathies were always with St. George and she was drawn further into politics when an introduction to Gladstone in 1887 set alight her campaigning zeal.

In the meantime she had given birth to a son, in December 1886. It is noteworthy that the future heir of the Grove baronetcy was not named Thomas or Walter in the traditional Grove way, but Gerald – a firm reminder that he was the son of 'Geraldine'. His was a difficult birth in a midwinter of great severity. On Boxing Day there was a heavy fall of snow and by the end of the year the country was completely snowed up. As with her first child she tried to breast-feed the baby but failed to do so adequately. A period of despondency followed when she was troubled with a rash – a recurring ailment of hers. She was fully recovered by the summer however, when she saw Queen Victoria's Jubilee procession from a vantage point in Lombard Street at the offices of the Phoenix Fire

Insurance company. Back home in August she enjoyed the annual gala day at the Larmer Tree where the band and the illuminations pleased her, and the family party 'danced about and had claret cup'.

At the beginning of October she went with Kathleen Grove (now Mrs. Edmund Mansel-Pleydell) to a great Liberal rally at Templecombe. An impressive army of speakers included two of their local friends, Lord Wolverton and Edwin Portman of Bryanston, but it was John Morley who made the deepest impression on Agnes. Within days she was planning to go to Nottingham to hear, as she described him, 'that great Grand Old Man, W.E.G.' The intention was to rèndezvous first with Walter, who was returning from a shooting party in Scotland, and with her brother, St. George, at a Nottingham hotel. As they habitually missed trains and misunderstood or misdirected telegrams, it is no surprise that Agnes eventually arrived at the hall alone, penniless and without a ticket for her seat on the platform. In such circumstances she was apt to set off a series of sparkling oscillations between panic and wrath which emitted an electrical discharge of notable force. Fortunately Lord Wolverton spotted her at this critical moment and took her in tow.

The outcome exceeded her wildest hopes. She was given a seat with Gladstone's party, heard 'the grandest speech ever heard' and was invited to dine with them afterwards. She sat beside Arnold Morley, the Liberal's chief whip, and soon learnt that Henry Gladstone and Lord Wolverton had arranged for her to travel in Mr. Gladstone's 'private special saloon train' to its next stop, Derby. She rode to the station in one of the procession of carriages that passed through cheering crowds, and once on board the train she was personally introduced to Gladstone: 'he shook me warmly by the hand and hoped I was not tired to which I replied, no, I would do still more to hear what I had heard'.

At twenty-four, and in the full flower of her beauty, Agnes must have been an attractive recruit to the party. A readiness to draw her into group photographs is understandable. At Derby there was again an enthusiastic reception for the procession of carriages driving through the streets. The Liberal member here was Sir William Harcourt, Chancellor of the Exchequer in Gladstone's recent administration. Both men made speeches at the town hall and Agnes sat opposite them at the subsequent lunch.

Walter meanwhile had wandered fruitlessly round Nottingham, found the hotels fully booked and gone home. What happened to St.

George remains a mystery. After the closing festivities at Derby Agnes saw no prospect of getting back to Berwick St. John that night so she returned to London with Henry Gladstone and Lord Wolverton. When Walter drove into Tisbury station the following afternoon to meet her off the London train there must have been a lot to talk about. Agnes had promised to attend Lord Wolverton's meeting at Wimborne in three days time but Walter persuaded her to stay at home with him. It was a sad decision, in the event: a fortnight later Lord Wolverton died suddenly.

Chapter Eleven

Agnes's devotion to Gladstone and the Liberal cause was sustained by an occasional encounter with the great man during the next two years after the triumphant visit to Nottingham and Derby. They met in Kensington at a bazaar – presumably a political fundraising bazaar. And when he toured Dorset in 1889 she rode in Sir Thomas's coach to Shaftesbury and Gillingham 'to see and hear G.O.M.' Agnes's daughter, Honor, now six years old, was privileged to present a basket of flowers to Mrs. Gladstone, whereupon Gladstone kissed Honor and said 'What a beautiful child'. Routine stuff for a political veteran, but faithfully recorded by Agnes in her journal. It was some consolation perhaps for Walter's defeat a few months earlier in a county council election.

Another political figure whom she had met at Nottingham became a closer acquaintance. This was Sir William Harcourt who lived in the New Forest, at Lyndhurst, and gave valuable support to Liberals in the adjacent constituencies of Dorset and Wiltshire. In the autumn of 1889 he made the principal speech at a Grand Meeting of Liberals at Salisbury, which Agnes attended. Afterwards he and the new Lord Wolverton drove with Sir Thomas to Ferne where they were to stay the night, as were Walter and Agnes. What followed is not clear but Agnes's account reads – 'Disgraceful scene outside. Sir W. Harcourt who was going to stay till tomorrow left suddenly. Ld. Wolverton also left'. There is no indication of who made the disgraceful scene, and Harcourt did not refer to it in the letter he wrote on his return home. He expressed himself as 'very glad if I have been of any service to the cause in Wilts.' and now looking forward to 'a respite for a time from the rumbling of the political wheels'. He concluded with friendly greetings to 'all your party and especially to Mrs. Grove a lady to whom I have long lost my heart.'

The scene at Ferne was calm in the following autumn when Sir Thomas threw open the park for a political meeting, at which the case for Irish Home Rule was presented eloquently by T.D. Sullivan M.P. Nothing like such a gathering had ever been seen in this quiet rural setting. The *Western Chronicle* reported every word of every speech, with illustrations and a history of the Grove family added for good measure.

The development of her political sympathies brought Agnes into closer harmony with Sir Thomas Grove and perhaps emphasised her alienation from her father. She spent more time with Sir Thomas and at Ferne, becoming more fully identified as a Grove. Her old home at Rushmore was still frequently visited and the ties of family affection with her brothers and sisters were strong, but the personality of the General makes surprisingly little impression on the record of her life that she committed to her diaries in the early years of her marriage. Her mother took an interest in Agnes's maternal and domestic preoccupations, but the General seems always to have stood apart in an impersonal way.

There is a vivid and somewhat chilling example of this in the winter of 1888/89. By December Agnes was six months' pregnant with her third child (Oenone, born the following March) and she was in debt and under pressure from creditors. Her diary entries are brief and not very revealing –

> Dec 1. I lunched at Rushmore and had talk £P [i.e. money with Papa]
>
> Dec 7. We lunched at Rushmore and went to Ferne, talked to Sir T. about money matters.
>
> Dec 9. I drove children up to Ferne. They were insulted.

The nature of the 'insult' is not disclosed, but the word signals very plainly that Agnes was on edge and acutely ready to take offence. On December 14 she wrote to her father – a letter of such a strange tone and character that it is worth reproducing in full.

> Dear Papa,
>
> I make one final appeal to you to know if you intend to fulfil yr distinct promise made to help me with the 'gifts' of money

beyond the £200 a year settled on me. You said to me the other day, that you were 'exceedingly sorry for the narrowness of our means', but that you had 'made a very liberal offer and that if Sir Thomas refused to accept it the odium rested with him'. Now since then Sir Thomas has consented to pay Walter's debts again, and in addition give him £50 a year more if you would do the same. But I cannot and will not ask him to pay *my* debts incurred solely on my own responsibility in the belief that you would keep your word when you told me of yr. own accord that you would from time to time give me gifts of money which would be equivalent to the £100 a year that you had withdrawn.

That you made this promise there is no denying as I have a letter from you in which you refer to it, reminding me that 'at yr. death these presents would of course cease', and which promise made you have given me no reason to suppose that through my conduct to you, or otherwise, you consider yr. self justified in breaking. You cannot blame *us* if we are unable to force Sir Thomas to sell his land, but rather on the contrary endeavour to reward us for the strenuous efforts we have made to induce him to do so.

As therefore I incurred these debts (which amount to a little under £100 and which consist entirely for clothing for myself and my children and which extend from the period – which is now over 2 years' – when you ceased to give me the extra £100 which was all the allowance I ever had to dress myself and my children, and which with an incresing family is the very least I can spend to keep them warmly and tidily clad) on the understanding that you would give me sufficient to pay them according to yr. word, I cannot see how you can honestly withold or *desire* to withold from me a sum sufficient to cover these debts thus incurred, the payment of which will alone prevent our having bailiffs in the house and that soon (as I have several summonses out against me already).

If you recognise the odium which would be attached to Sir Thomas were he to neglect to help his son to the extent that lay in his power *without* having made any promise, to help him beforehand, you will surely recognise the same responsibility to help yr. daughter (to whom you *did* make a distinct promise) in the present immediate difficulty and also make some small

> provision *well* within the possibility of yr. means to provide against absolute want in the future, and what you yourself recently stigmatised as an 'impossible and miserable state of things'.
>
> I need only add that, should you answer this appeal in the manner that I cannot but hope you will inevitably do, I on my part will not fail to recognise it with all filial gratitude and due appreciation.
>
> Yr. affectn daughter
>
> Agnes G. Grove

It may sound like the language of prosecuting counsel rather than a daughter, but it is sadly typical of their relationship at this time. Two months later they were in a fresh dispute, involving Agnes's brother Willy. Now thirty years old, and with service in the Zulu war and in the Sudan behind him, Willy had decided to marry. He came to Berwick to tell Agnes that he had proposed and was now engaged. His intended bride was a stranger to the family – 'Miss Muriel Mildmay, whom we none of us know but he seems in earnest', Agnes wrote, adding 'I hope it will answer'.

The General did not approve of Miss Mildmay. Willy's satisfactory career in the General's old regiment and his amenably conformist nature made him a particular favourite with his father, who had more exalted matrimonial aspirations for him. Willy seems to have defended his action by invoking the name of Agnes as a supporter: Miss Mildmay had been encouraged to write to Agnes, and Agnes had replied. This was enough to stir the General to an angry accusation of meddling. As Agnes was within a fortnight almost of her confinement Walter took it upon himself to reply –

> My dear General, You are quite wrong in supposing Agnes wishes or advised Willy to make an improvident marriage. I have seen her letters in answer to Miss Mildmay's and think them judicious and *not in the least* calculated to encourage the Mildmay family to force their daughter's suit on Willy.

Poor Miss Mildmay! She lost her Willy who, four years later, married a niece of Lady Fitzgerald – 'Blossie' Payne.

These abrasive family exchanges may perhaps be reckoned an almost normal currency, year in year out, but they alternated with moods of close affection and loyalty and with the closing of ranks that responds to deeper tragedies. On the day after Walter's letter to the General, news came that Lionel had again come back from Canada and was 'in a shocking state of health'. Mrs. Pitt-Rivers went hurrying to London to meet him and care for him. In the following year Agnes had yet more alarming news of her youngest brother, Arthur, and turned instinctively to her father –

> I had yesterday the most dreadful letter from Alice telling me of Arthur's terrible condition, and I waited at Tisbury hearing Papa was coming. He told me much sad news that I had not heard before. How the poor boy has constantly to have two keepers with him and how he tries to escape. I can think of nothing else, it quite upsets me. I so long to get to him and try what I can do. If they could only get him into the country it would be so much better for him.

That was early in June 1890. Later in the month she saw Arthur several times in London, when he was in the care of a doctor but came to 4 Grosvenor Gardens and probably stayed there. Agnes recorded that she saw him nearly every day at one stage – either at their London home or at the doctor's establishment. There seems to have been a family conference: the General came up to London and St. George came to lunch when Arthur also was present. In the summer, when Agnes and some of the family were holidaying at Weymouth, Arthur joined them there; and when Agnes saw him again in London she thought him 'very strong and well and quite rational'. In October he turned up unexpectedly during a tennis party at Rushmore.

Some undated correspondence suggests that St. George had been trying, through his business contacts, to settle Arthur down in quiet employment with a Mr. Crompton of the Arc Works at Chelmsford. In a letter to his father Arthur wrote

> I must believe that you would like me to lead a useful life. I have now a great opening – an opportunity of working and learning in the most interesting and useful business (I think) there is. Mr. Crompton has written saying it would be a pity for me to leave his works so soon and proposes my going there until the 18 months are expired, being 6 or 7 months longer. Therefore I have settled to go back tomorrow and try and make the best of my time.
>
> You have already acquiesced in the trial. It is of great importance I should not lose time now – such an opportunity

> may not occur again. If at the end of 18 months I see no prospects of being successful I shall be ready to shift my course to something else.

It seems that the arrangement with Mr. Crompton was some kind of apprenticeship, perhaps involving a premium or a forfeit, and that Arthur's condition caused a premature termination. What is certain is that Mr. Crompton demanded £150 from St. George, and was prepared to sue for it. The General was not eager to foot the bill and resented a report that Aunt Maude had said he ought to do so. His aggrieved letter to her has not survived, but her reply has. As one might expect of Aunt Maude it is polite, firm and crushing –

> 'I do not remember arguing to Lionel that you ought to pay the £150 to W. Crompton that St. George is bound to pay in 3 months for Arthur; I did say to Lionel I hoped he would explain to you the circumstances thro' which St. George found himself liable for that sum, namely his unwillingness to go into the witness box to have to let the public know that Arthur was in a lunatic asylum, and I said to St. George that I thought he was right to avoid such a disclosure. I am most sorry that St. George shd have forfeited your goodwill by any disrespect and disregard of yr. wishes.

In March 1891 Arthur went voluntarily into an institution at Dumfries, after a trip to Algiers accompanied by a Mr. Bright had failed to improve his health. He was unhappy at Dumfries, and only a month later he tried to escape but was recaptured after two days, unhurt but shaken after falling down a railway embankment. He was then formally certified as insane.

Worry as she might over Arthur's condition, her own ill-health and her financial difficulties, Agnes of course had brighter and happier episodes in the late eighties and early nineties. There were the spring and summer expeditions to be enjoyed: to Weymouth for the Yeomanry Review and the yachting, to the Ascot Races which combined so usefully with visits to Walter's sister, Edith Foster, at Clewer and to Agnes's sister, Ursula Scott, at Thorpe, and of course to London for the balls and theatre-going that were an essential part of the 'Season'.

In this annual blending of pleasures a particularly subtle and scarcely defined spice was added by the attentions of certain gentlemen who might be described as Agnes's *beaux*. She had enjoyed her flirtations before she married Walter and she did not forswear them afterwards. At Weymouth and at Ascot George Dawson-Damer and Mr. Chandos Pole were agreeably attentive. References to them in her diaries are laconic, but their frequency does become noticeable. Her liking for Dawson-Damer dated back to her teens when she had had an adolescent 'crush' on him. He married in 1881 and became Viscount Carlow in 1889. At Weymouth in May of that latter year Agnes noted on the day of her arrival 'Saw G.D. Damer now Lord Carlow': the words 'and Lady' were inserted as an afterthought. Next day's entry includes 'Lord C'. and the following day's account of a ball records 'danced Ld. C' and mentions nobody else. At the next day's claypigeon shoot she betted in penny points with Mr. E. Farquharson & Lord Carlow. The following afternoon there were sports and 'Lord Carlow did well'. After which everyone left Weymouth. However there was Ascot to come: here she had tea with Lord Carlow, walked down to the booths with him and 'he played the fool and insisted on our being photographed'.

It is impossible to say how earnest or how flippant these relationships may have been. There is no denying that, at different stages of her life, Agnes's diary gives a certain significance to one or two men. Occasionally an unmistakeable emotional tension reveals itself in a quarrel, but there are two good reasons for caution in interpreting such moments. Each generation decides in its own manner how to conduct these marginal fondnesses and our own customs may be very different from those of an earlier generation. Further, there is no reason to doubt Agnes's abiding devotion to Walter. He must have been a monotonous companion for he evidently subscribed to his father's creed that a day was wasted if he did not shoot or hunt something before the sun went down. Yet even late in life, and at times when he was most exasperating, the warmth and sincerity of Agnes's affection for him is undeniable. Perhaps no more need be said than that Agnes was a highly attractive woman who aroused men's admiration, expected it – and revelled in it.

At a homelier level one or two pleasant little scenes stand out during this period. In February 1890 the General, in pursuit of his scientific interests, arranged for a Mr. Lind to demonstrate a phonograph at Rushmore and give a lecture about this astonishing invention. On the first day the company consisted of members of the family and guests staying at Rushmore. Next day all the tenants and tradespeople were invited. Agnes went on both days and judged it 'most interesting'.

That year ended in a white Christmas. On December 16 'snow began again', Agnes noted. On the 19th, when she and the children were at Rushmore, 'snow storm began. We all went out and they made a huge snow-bear'. Next day snow continued to fall heavily and by the 21st when she and the General walked as far as the lodge, there were two snowploughs at work. The question now was how to get the children back home to Berwick St. John for Christmas Day. Agnes's description of events on the 22nd gives a charming picture of an adventure the children must have long remembered.

> We all left Rushmore after luncheon – Gerald and Oenone in panniers on the pony, Honor riding the donkey, the luggage in pack saddles. I went with Papa as far as the top of the hill. Miss Nixon rode my horse to there and then I rode the rest of the way home. The road was completely blocked in parts.

Miss Nixon was the children's governess and was due to go on holiday. Agnes had engaged her in July, to replace Estelle, and she lasted a year. Her final departure distressed Honor and claims attention now for one of the stronger undercurrents of Agnes's life – the recurring crisis that the upper classes had to face in what they referred to as 'the servant problem'. Given their way of life it was a real and increasing problem. They reckoned to entertain lavishly, to travel from house-party to house-party and to delegate the care of their infants from a very early age. That was the customary way of life to which they had been reared and for which they had the material resources. The typical economy of the aristocratic establishment required an inexhaustible supply of butlers, cooks, nurses, governesses, coachmen, gardeners, gamekeepers, grooms and the like. A photo of only the indoor staff at Ferne looks like a football team. Agnes and Walter were among the poorer members of their class, and were often desperately short of ready money, but they considered an indoor staff of five as necessary. Agnes's 1888 diary has some revealing notes pencilled in the back, indicating annual wages for governess (£20), a nurse (£12), a maid (£20), a parlourmaid (£16) and a cook (£22). Another list names four women – Estelle, a governess and Miss Nixon's predecessor (£22), Alice (£22), Clara (£15) and Elise (£10) – an annual cost of £69 which is verified by a separate note 'wages quarterly £17/5/–'. A further note reads 'my pin money £100'.

Domestic service may have been a form of abject servitude in the 'bad old days' – whenever they were – but by the last quarter of the nineteenth century the balance of advantage was beginning to shift noticeably in favour of the servant. Demand was outstripping supply, as every little middle class household in the growing cities insisted on having its own servants. Registry offices sprang up to meet this demand, and servants were correspondingly less afraid of the consequences of dismissal. They would soon find another job and possibly a better one.

Agnes liked to devote her attention exclusively to each newly born child for the first month of its life, subsequently delegating the routines of infancy to nurse and governess. She liked to entertain friends and relatives at luncheon and dinner whenever she was at home, and to accommodate guests – expected or unexpected – for as many nights as they chose to stay. When she went away she would be likely to take her personal maid with her. It was all a part of the open-house tradition established before the coming of railways and hotels and motorcars. Given Agnes's imperious temper it is not surprising to find her writing in her diary –

> November 7. Heard from Mrs. Oppenheim nurse we engaged not coming. Said mother was dying. I went up to London again, called at all the places and went to unearth the woman in the hole she lived in. Found no one there.
>
> November 8. Went to see a Mrs. Gillespie about a girl I saw, having put an advertisement in Morning Post and spent eight shillings in cabs. Girl engaged [sc. by someone else]. Went to see Mrs. Brattley and saw another girl who promised to come – and others. Got quite desperate, none can imagine the dreary dreadful time I went through. It seemed so hopeless, trying to get a nurse, and I had been through so much discomfort and disagreeableness for not having a proper one that I was *most* unhappy. Walter, expecting me back every day, naturally did not write and altogether it was *dreadful*.
>
> November 9. Went again Mrs. Gillespie. Kind woman – then went on to house to see why girl not come.
>
> November 10. Still in despair. Heard of another girl, went to see her.
>
> November 11. Saw another girl at Eaton Terrace, also nuns and others. Had great trouble to get her. Went four times to the house and finally triumphed.

In the circumstances *triumph* is scarcely too strong a word for this tenacious stalking of a quarry more elusive than the stag or hare or partridge to which Walter and Sir Thomas addressed their hunting instincts.

And then there were cooks, as always a class apart. There was the occasion, for instance, when Lord Alington asked Agnes to put him up at Berwick for a night or two over New Year's Eve. Being without a cook at the time Agnes telegraphed to E. Townsend to come urgently. Next day E. Townsend arrived, but within three days Agnes recorded sadly 'Cook dreadful'. A more temperamental cook was J. Baker who arrived in July 1891 a few days after 'Sara Woodbine, black nurse who seems nice' had joined the household. The departure of J. Baker a mere six days later stirred Agnes to a graphic report in her diary –

> In morning cook was insolent. When told that she had better go out of the house, if she could not behave, went to the Rectory in hysterics. Refused to go back and walked all over the county and to Bests where she was when I went to tea.

The dawning of the nineties was to accelerate social change in various ways. Like so many people in a time of transition Agnes fought sometimes on one side and sometimes on the other. She believed that cooks and nursemaids should be respectful and know their place. She also thought they should have the vote, and she was to play her part in that cause. Meanwhile she was becoming aware of other new trends. In the spring of '91 Agnes was having tea with Aunt Maude and others at Dover Street when Blanche Hogan came in. 'She's separated from her husband', Agnes recorded, 'it created a sensation'. The following evening Agnes paid a thought-provoking visit to the theatre: she saw the first London production of Ibsen's *Hedda Gabler*.

Chapter Twelve

In the summer of 1891 Agnes went to a garden party, noting afterwards 'Miss Kennedy the soothsayer there. I went in and she told me my character very truly & said something would happen within 5 weeks to change my whole life'. Eagerly one turns the next few pages of Agnes's diary to see if Miss Kennedy did indeed say sooth. Alas, it was an unusually humdrum period of children's parties, family luncheons and frustrating searches for employable cooks. Nothing happened to change Agnes's way of life in any immediate and recognisable particular.

The one novelty that might be discerned was the lightly superstitious impulse that led her to pay any attention to Miss Kennedy. A few days later a guest at Ferne whiled away an evening telling fortunes with cards, and it became the craze of the moment: twice more within a week there were fortune telling sessions at Ferne. It is the lightest of straws in the wind but it catches the mood of the nineties. The pious churchgoing and family prayers of Agnes's childhood needed now the elasticity to admit the new cults of magic and 'psychic' divination. In a letter dated October 3, 1892, Agnes wrote 'I also do pencil-writing and write away like fun but crystal-seeing I am no good at'. By 'pencil-writing' she meant spirit-writing by the method usually associated with the ouija-board or *planchette*. Her brother, St. George, meanwhile became deeply engaged in psychical research: in a later entry she recorded that he had been invited to Stockholm 'to investigate a spook'.

As the phrase suggests, these voyages of discovery into the realm of the supernatural and the paranormal were engaging acts of folly in the main, so far as Agnes was concerned – a kind of entertainment while the vogue lasted. There were more practical and urgent novelties to seize her deeper attention. It was in the nineties that Victorian England lost its nerve and opened its doors to the new ideas it might have hoped to exclude. Many traditional attitudes were now under scrutiny and subject to revision – in politics, in morals, in religion, in the arts and in social etiquette. As the decade unfolded Agnes entered those areas of public controversy where women were increasingly active. She was a member of the Council of the Women's Liberal Federation. She appeared in *tableaux* at Queen's Gate Hall in London in aid of women's suffrage, and became president of the Forward Suffrage Union. She spoke against vivisection and against vaccination. In short, she evolved her own personal version of the New Woman. And at home in Wiltshire, while Walter fulfilled his traditional role on the magistrate's bench, Agnes was busy gaining experience of local government on the Board of Guardians, characteristically proposing the admission of the Press to all their meetings – a proposal that was heavily defeated.

Where the soothsayer might have been more explicit was in the realm of Agnes's personal feelings and family relationships, for it was a fair bet that her impetuous emotional nature would continue to express itself in sudden passionate flashes of anger or of tenderness. At the centre of her life were Walter and their three children, Honor, Gerald and Oenone. Next to them came the two family establishments, Rushmore and Ferne, with their everchanging pattern of squabbles and reconciliations and their firm underlying loyalties. The importance of this inner private world of kinship was always paramount. As the years passed Walter might seem to drift into obscurity, increasingly overshadowed by Agnes's activities, but he was the secure anchorage to which she always returned and her love for him was powerfully felt. A letter she wrote to him – calling him by his pet-name 'Fard' – in 1891 when he was sailing at Cowes is eloquent in its testimony –

My darling Fard,

I don't know where you are but my heart goes out with a desire to write to you. When I am here quite alone by myself as I have been today I think so much of you Fard, and all I ever think only makes my heart yearn *tenderly* towards you, so much so that I can't imagine myself quietly as I sometimes try, ever getting irritated with and irritated at you. I say to myself, what is there in my dear good gentle loving considerate kind precious Fard that can make me ever feel otherwise than as I do now, *so* fond tender and affectionate. I know I never could live here without you. Everything that reminds me of you sends a little sort of *pang* to my heart, now when I know you will soon be here again; but if I knew you never would come back, what would it be *then*. You always *say* you are fonder of me than I am of you, but I do not think you are *really*. It's only in a sort of more passionate "manny" way that you are; you do not think so much of me when I am not there, or if you do you never tell me so in yr letters, and if you did you *would* because you know how it would please me. You used to before we married but now the *romance* has gone out of yr love but not out of mine. Tell me if you don't think so, and if you ever have 'pangs' when something suddenly reminds you of me.

I took the children all up to Rushmore yesterday. Ursula & her 3 children are there and Alice and her 3 children, so there were 9 grandchildren all together. P.R. [her father] said he thought I was 'looking very ill' as usual! That I must take care and 'lie up'. What for? He is very excited about the picture.

We are just off to pic-nic at the Larmer. I am so glad you are enjoying yr. sail. It will do my dear heart good.

Ever ever yr

Dills.

'Dills' was one of her pet-names: 'Moz' was another. The picture that pleased General Pitt-Rivers was the portrait of Agnes he had commissioned from the distinguished portrait painter of the period, Fred Beaumont. It was exhibited at the Royal Academy in 1892.

Her father's concern about her health was not as misplaced as Agnes imagined. The early 1890s were a period of physical strain and recurring illness for her. She was seriously ill with peritonitis in 1892 and a protracted convalescence was accompanied with relapses and the passing of a gall-stone. Her doctor feared she might suffer a permanently enlarged and diseased liver. The following year she gave birth to a second son, Terence, and two years later she was again pregnant.

Some of the more tempestuous moments within the family circle probably arose from these bouts of stress and sickness. A particularly unwelcome ailment to which Agnes was subject was a facial rash. In 1891, for instance, she put on a thick veil before going into Hyde Park. She met Walter's sister, Kate, and Molly Langley 'who was offensive'. The storm signals are unmistakable. A few days later she saw Kate with her husband, Eddy Pleydell, 'and had a row but they all lied so I am quit of the lot for good, which is a good thing'.

Sadly the breach with Kate persisted for some time. When they met at Rushmore three months later Agnes would not speak to her. Another and more mysterious explosion centred on Willy, whose military duties spared him to spend some time at Rushmore during the hunting season in 1891. He owned a horse called Arabic which he sometimes allowed Agnes to ride, to her great delight.

> I went out hunting on Arabic, with Walter on Jack Benett's chestnut, at Iwerne. Most exciting day. Arabic went beautifully. Enjoyed myself very much. Got bad cut under chin when jumping huge blind fence, many of which I went over during the day.

Later that year she went up to Rushmore and rode Arabic with Willy and their younger brother, Douglas, to Fontmell; after which she rode him home to keep, 'Willy having kindly given him to me'. When Willy married, in the spring of 1893, Agnes's children were conspicuously present – Oenone as bridesmaid, Gerald as page. But when Willy and his bride came to Rushmore in the summer and Agnes took her two eldest children to a family luncheon there, 'most unpleasant and disgraceful scenes took place'. What precisely happened is not disclosed, but it must have been a memorable set-piece in the family tradition and thereafter a coolness towards Willy persisted.

It was with St. George, among her brothers, that Agnes seemed to have the easiest comradeship. His special blend of inventive genius, magnanimity and plain dottiness drew from her an affectionate admiration. It was a sad day when she heard, in March 1892, that he had lost a court action intended to enforce his patents for electric lighting. As far back as 1878 he had invented the Lane Fox system and taken out one of the earliest patents for the use of small incandescent lamps in parallel. It is said that Edison himself conceded that St. George's invention of the carbon filament was the decisive factor in the commercial development of electric light. However, the action was lost and the fortune that St. George so nearly secured passed into other pockets, while he could not find the money to pay for his lodgings.

Later in the year he stayed at Berwick while Walter was away. The bitterness and despair that might be expected are wholly absent from the account of her brother that Agnes gave in a letter to Walter. Instead there is an irrepressible whimsicality.

> My Darling Fard,
>
> I have much to tell you. I am really much better, practically free from pain. I had a bath today by "the doctor's!" orders (you know what that means). Then Mama brought me £10, so that will help. But I don't pay my journey, mind. I am going to pay some old bills and threatened summonses.
>
> Then I have more news. St. George has proposed to Coralie because he felt he had 'drifted' thitherwards. Joyfully accepted – but – he says he felt he had raised the girl's hopes! so was bound to do the honourable thing, but she says she can't quite give up her religion and wished St. G. to "agree to differ". This he says he never will do and they must think alike or it is no marriage. Then her family it is supposed will sneer at her for marrying a pauper – but he says his debts could be financed before the marriage! Then again he feels he has done the right thing as he went to stay there! Otherwise it might occasion the enemy to blaspheme!
>
> So that's how the matter rests. I do not think there has been a public announcement made yet, but I asked him straight. The foregoing statement was the answer. Coralie he believes is devoted to him and has been for years! St. George says, having sent her the Kreutzer Sonata, he is perhaps bound to marry her!

In the event he did not marry Coralie. He remained a bachelor until 1899 when he married the Marquess of Queensberry's daughter, Lady Edith Douglas.

Another side of St. George's character which must have endeared him to Agnes was his concern for their brother, Arthur. During his confinement at Dumfries Arthur's condition deteriorated and it was decided to move him to Malling Place in Kent. While he was being transferred he escaped and made his way to 4 Grosvenor Gardens, where he retired to bed. Agnes meanwhile had come to London for the wedding of her cousin, Edith Fox, bringing Honor as one of the bridesmaids. After a theatre and a late supper at the Bachelors Club Agnes stayed the night, to be awakened with the news that Arthur was missing.

> He slept in the house for a short time – escaped again early this morning and was brought back. Then we had a terrible morning. He locked himself in twice and was finally got off at about 12. I was with him about an hour. He looks terribly changed and ill but went off happily. Douglas and Walt went to the station with him.

That was in 1893, when his sad life had not much longer to run. The onset of tuberculosis was to terminate it. In 1895 St. George wrote to General Pitt-Rivers urging him to move Arthur to Bournemouth –

> Even tho' he may be past recovery, the change wd probably relieve him and make his last days happier. The place has great attraction for him. I am told that it is the usual effect of tuberculosis to clear the mind.

It was too late, however. Within a week Arthur was dead. The General brought his body to Tollard Royal for burial in the churchyard, with a Celtic cross as his headstone.

Outside the family circle Agnes continued to enjoy her customary round of social visits. Two of them she describes fully enough to help us to imagine what the house-parties of the nineties were like. The first was a relatively local one, at Rhinefield House in the New Forest: the second a grander affair at the vice-regal lodge in Dublin.

Rhinefield House was a newly built mansion of impressive vulgarity near Brockenhurst and adjoining the Ornamental Drive, which is a celebrated feature of the Forest. The owners of the house were the Walker-Munros, the husband being the Lionel Munro who was one of Agnes's earliest admirers. The younger son of a baronet, Lionel joined the Royal Navy and was wounded in the Sudan in 1885 before marrying Mabel Zoe Walker, the heiress of a wealthy industrialist. He added his wife's family name to his own, and with her fortune he was able to build not only Rhinefield House but also St. Saviour's church, which was reputedly commissioned after a quarrel with the incumbent of Brockenhurst's existing parish church.

Agnes and Walter travelled by train to Brockenhurst on a Tuesday afternoon in January, to stay with their friends for the rest of the week. They arrived about seven o'clock and sat down to dinner as a party of seventeen. Lionel was Agnes's escort – 'by fair choosing', she recorded. The following morning they were photographed and went skating; after which Agnes became involved in a political argument with Lady Carew and a Mr. Wood. In the evening there was a ball.

On Thursday Walter went off with two of the party to shoot rabbits, while Agnes took an afternoon stroll with Lionel and some other guests. She and Lionel 'went off for fun to take a short cut and got lost and did not come back till after tea'. In the evening they rehearsed the tableaux which were to be the great event of the visit.

The final evening was given over to 'theatricals' after a day of rehearsals. There was a play, *The Duchess of Bayswater*, and there were the tableaux. Agnes's role was as Marie Antoinette. Mrs. Walker-Munro exercised a hostess's right to appear as Beauty in 'Beauty and the Beast', a part for which she seems not to have been ideally suited. The programme culminated in dancing, and next morning the guests dispersed.

The visit to Dublin took place two years later, in 1895. The Viceroy was Robert Monckton Milnes, Lord Houghton (who shortly afterwards became Marquis of Crewe). Like his father he was a man of literary interests and one of his earliest invitations to visit Dublin had gone to Thomas Hardy. As a result of that visit one of Lord Houghton's sisters, Florence Henniker, had developed a close friendship with Hardy.

Lord Houghton had first met Agnes in 1894 at a rather grand dinner party given by Mary Jeune, with the Duke of Teck among the guests. Lady Jeune was Agnes's aunt by marriage: when she married Sir Francis Jeune she was the widow of John Stanley. As a London hostess she blended actors, authors and artists with the nobility in what was still a somewhat novel mixture. Hardy was a frequent guest and 'lodger'. Irving and Ellen Terry would join peers and Cabinet ministers at her table.

The party that Lord Houghton invited to Dublin had a distinctly 'Stanley' flavour. Lady Jeune herself was there and beside Agnes her eldest brother Alex Pitt-Rivers was invited. So too was Lord Stanley's heir, Lyulph Stanley. Walter of course was included as was Alex's wife, Ruth (a daughter of Lord Henry Thynne who had married Alex in 1889). The role of hostess was taken on this occasion not by Mrs. Henniker but by her eldest sister, Lady Fitzgerald.

The entries in Agnes's diary are laconic but they give the impression that Lord Houghton was uncommonly attentive to her. On the first night there was a levée, with a band playing and she sat next to the Viceroy at supper. Her diary continues –

> Feb 13. Long talk in morning with His Ex[cellency]. Walked in town with Walter in morning. Drove Viceregal Lodge in afternoon. Drove back with Lord H. Drawing-room in evening.
>
> Feb 14. Heard that Grandmama was very ill. Afraid we should have to go. Had tea [at the] Wolseleys. Went to Lord H's room. He gave me his book of poems. Dance-dinner in the evening.
>
> Feb 15. Went and looked at photographs in library. Chose one. Dinner and dance in evening in St. Patrick's Hall. Most delightful evening of all.
>
> Feb 16. Went round the town to shops with Captan Jekyll. Saw nothing. Sat next to Lord H at dinner and talked after. [in the heavy square brackets that indicate mourning she has added 'Grandmama died at 4 o'clock this morning'].
>
> Feb 17. Read in morning, went for a walk – stables and round gardens after. Then to see books. Went in to dinner with His Ex. Played games in evening.

Next morning she left Dublin and felt ill on the journey back to England – hardly surprising as she was extremely pregnant. Her ill-health persisted into March, cheered momentarily by a present from Lord Houghton of a volume of his translations. On March 25 she gave birth to a baby boy. Two days later she wrote 'This morning the greatest sorrow of my life happened to me. At 9.00 my beautiful baby died'.

Chapter Thirteen

After the death of her baby Agnes virtually stopped writing in her diary for some weeks. Many days were left blank, while others recorded only a bare note of the names of those who called on her. Throughout April, 1895, she must have been physically weak and numb with grief. By May, however, she was becoming active again. She took part in a political meeting locally, with Walter in the chair, and then went to London for the conference of Liberal women. She spent three days at the conference and saw her redoubtable Stanley aunts, Rosalind and Maude. She also called on the Jeunes and attended a royal 'drawing-room'. Before leaving London at the beginning of June, she went twice to the House of Commons for debates on the Factory Bill, hearing speeches by Burns, Asquith and George Wyndham.

Her return to Berwick was brief. She went to Ascot as usual and spent a further month in London, going several times to hear Mrs. Besant and once to a lecture at the Psychical Research Society. During July a General Election sent her back to Wiltshire to help Walter's father in the defence of his seat, but to no avail – he lost by a narrow margin of 26 votes. In London once more she renewed and strengthened the friendships she had made in Dublin. Taking tea at Aunt Maude's she met again the Viceroy's sister, Lady Fitzgerald, and their younger sister, the Hon. Mrs. Henniker. The following day Agnes had luncheon with Lord Houghton (now the newly created Marquis of Crewe) and his two sisters; after which he walked back to Smith Square with her. In August, while visiting Walter's cousin Aimée de Hoghton, Agnes met Lord Crewe again at York

Races. It needs no great flight of fancy to imagine that on one of these occasions the conversation ranged over the literary events of the day, and more particularly the current fame of Thomas Hardy. He had collaborated with Mrs. Henniker in a short story, 'The Spectre of the Real', which had been published in the previous November, and his latest serial was currently appearing in *Harpers New Monthly Magazine* – though it had not yet acquired its ultimate title, *Jude the Obscure*.

When Agnes went home after York Races she would have been interested to learn that Hardy and his wife were expected to arrive at Rushmore the following Tuesday for a short visit. The General's invitation was obviously timed to coincide with the annual Fête in the Larmer Tree Gardens. The two men would have known each other as fellow-members of the Athenaeum and Hardy had been a guest at 4 Grosvenor Gardens; Rushmore and Max Gate are within a couple of dozen miles of each other; and Hardy would have known about the rising popularity of this new Wessex folk-festival and might understandably like to witness it with its creator.

The daytime events were races of various kinds – on foot, on bicycles and on horses – on a course prepared beside the Gardens. There were music and singing in the open-air theatre and a party of Kentucky minstrels. And as the evening light faded the thousands of Vauxhall lamps were lit and a band played for dancing. The General's houseparty dined in the Gardens and Agnes joined them there. According to Hardy's account the dances were mostly polka-mazurkas and schottisches, until he and Agnes started some country dances. From early childhood Hardy had been reared in the musical tradition of country dancing and was accomplished as both a fiddler and a dancer: in later life he looked back on the evening in the Larmer Tree Gardens as the last occasion of its kind – the last measure he trod on the greensward, to use his own words. It was a romantic moment. In a letter to Mrs. Henniker a few days later Hardy described it as 'the most romantic time I have had since I visited you at Dublin'.

Students of Hardy's character will relish the irony of his comment. The visit to Dublin had initiated Hardy's romantic devotion to Mrs. Henniker which flowered in the years 1893-95 to a close friendship. Estranged as he was from his wife Hardy had looked to Mrs. Henniker for the emotional consolation that he needed. He had fostered her literary ambitions and seen himself as her mentor. 'The

Spectre of the Real' was the public expression of the partnership between master and pupil.

By the summer of 1895 the widening divergence of their attitudes on fundamental issues was evident, and with it the cooling of Hardy's ardour. A nostalgic regret had begun to tinge his letters to Mrs. Henniker: what had once seemed in prospect was no longer so. It was in that mood that Hardy came to Rushmore. Sitting and watching the dancing, a man in his mid-fifties who was easily moved by music and by romantic circumstances, he found a sympathetic response in the undeniably beautiful daughter of his host. Perhaps he talked to her about his boyhood experiences, playing second fiddle to his father's first and learning from his father a great repertoire of rustic dance tunes. How appropriate it would then be to call to the General's musicians to strike up one of the old tunes, and for Hardy and Agnes to invite others to follow their lead.

In some such way began the scene that Hardy recalled, over thirty years later, when he avowed his wish to have over again

> That old romance,
> And sit apart in the shade as we sat then
> After the dance
> The while I held her hand, and, to the booms
> Of contrabassos, feet still pulsed from the distant rooms.

It might be expected that they would meet again the following day but they did not. Agnes and Walter caught a morning train to London, and Agnes went on alone – except for the company of her personal maid, Davis – to Paris and Geneva, where she was to spend a restful holiday in the mountains near Chamonix with some friends and the family of her younger sister, Alice Lubbock. Of the Fête at the Larmer Tree gardens her diary records – 'Went to Larmer Tree sports, met and talked to Thomas Hardy, found him interesting. Dined there'. There is no reference to the dancing.

Hardy and his wife stayed one more night at Rushmore and then travelled back to Dorchester. It had been a pleasant visit, Hardy wrote to Florence Henniker, 'notwithstanding the trying temper of the hostess'. He liked the situation of Rushmore, 'high up on the Wiltshire downs', which suited him eminently. The lower altitude of Dorchester made him feel quite languid, on his return.

Agnes was back in England at the beginning of October. She had largely lost interest in her diary which says little about the remainder of the year; however it is clear that she started to write an article in connection with some controversy of the time. As there is no evidence that she had done anything of the kind before it is not unreasonable to assume that Hardy had encouraged her to do so. He had also promised to send her a copy of *Jude the Obscure* when it appeared in book form, so it was his intention to continue the acquaintanceship begun at the Larmer Tree. She sent him her article and on November 3 – two days after the publication of *Jude* – he replied in a kindly and considerate letter. He thought her work 'spirited and sincerely written' but showing signs of inexperience, 'as is natural enough'. He offered to mark the places that he considered faulty and suggested that she should rewrite the piece and return it to him so that he could send it to the appropriate editor. He thoughtfully added a warning that 'editors consider their own convenience and advantage only' and she must therefore 'not feel hurt if he returns it'. For the guidance of a novice the letter is an admirable piece of advice. It ended as follows –

> I have often thought of the pleasant conversation we had at the Larmer, and shall hope to renew it some day.
>
> I am sending, as I promised, a copy of my new book 'Jude the Obscure' for your acceptance. You are, I know, sufficiently broad of view to estimate without bias a tragedy of very unconventional lives.
>
> Ever sincerely Yours,
>
> Thomas Hardy.

A week later he wrote to Mrs. Henniker, somewhat lamely, 'my hesitating to send *Jude* was not because I thought you narrow – but because I had rather bored you with him during the writing of some of the story, or thought I had'. The plain truth was that Mrs. Henniker seemed to Hardy to echo, if in a milder form, the disapproval that Mrs. Hardy felt for the book; and he hoped for a more favourable response from Agnes.

Her reply was prompt. She liked *Jude* and she wanted Hardy to correct her article in the way he had suggested. Equally promptly he did so 'in a perfectly brutal manner', adding 'I am sure that the person who had intelligence enough to write it will know quite well that, if she goes in for literature – where competition is so keen and ruthless – it is truest friendship which points out faults frankly at starting'. A week later he had her rewritten piece back in his hands and despatched it to the editor of the *Atlantic Monthly* with a covering letter designed to 'quicken his reading of your essay'. This was a form of sponsorship which Hardy had previously given to some of the short stories of Mrs. Henniker, as he did later to the writings of Florence Dugdale who became his second wife.

On this immediate occasion Hardy's influence with editors did not prevail. On December 20 he had to forward to Agnes a letter of rejection, and again his sensitivity in handling a novice is endearing. 'You must not be out of heart about it,' he wrote, explaining that the decision would not spring from the merits or demerits of her work but would turn on editorial policy and topicality. The material could be reshaped and used later, and he added generously 'I wish the rejected MS had been mine, and not yours!'

During their correspondence Agnes had referred to the scene in *Jude* where Sue reproached herself for being too honest and yet not honest enough in her talk with little Time. As a mother of four children Agnes had a practical interest in the question of what facts should be told to children, or witheld from them, by their parents. Hardy now picked up this point and proposed that she should make it the subject of her next effort.

Her diary for the early months of 1896 throws no light on her response to his suggestion. Her health was poor: in mid-January she passed a gall-stone, and she had spells of recurring weakness. She recorded that Lord Crewe had sent her two volumes of Rossetti's poems but made no reference to any correspondence with Hardy. Towards the end of March she paid a brief visit to London, of which Hardy must have had foreknowledge. She arrived at 4 Grosvenor Gardens on March 23 to attend a tea-party next day at the Sesame Club in connection with the Education League. However she was feeling ill when she arrived in London and her doctor made her stay in bed. She therefore missed the Sesame party but got up on the following day when, she noted, 'Mr. Thomas Hardy came to see me. Also saw Aunt Maude.' Two days later she left London.

It was the first opportunity she and Hardy had had to meet since their dance at the Larmer Tree. On April 27 Hardy wrote to her, again encouraging her to complete the article on 'What children should be told' that he believed she contemplated writing. Rather strangely his letter gave no indication that he had visited her less than a fortnight previously. He must have seen or heard a draft of the article as he now advised her to shorten the section on Religion, and he offered to read her completed work.

Agnes took him at his word and her draft passed rapidly to and fro between them during the next two weeks, with Hardy pencilling 'ruthlessly' and curbing her tendency to become diffuse or go off at a tangent. He was of course in his element at such times – very much the seasoned professional who delighted in polishing and subediting and revising. His comment that her essay showed a sustained power of reasoning 'not usual in women's arguments' was perhaps less than tactful to an ardent champion of women's rights, but she must have recognised the genuine complimentary warmth with which he concluded – 'You are such a good little pupil that it is a pleasure to offer you suggestions'.

By the end of April the final touches had been added and Hardy sent Agnes's typescript to the editor of *Free Review*, judging him to be more tolerant of Agnes's unorthodox religious views than the more conventional editor of the *New Review*. While they waited for a decision Hardy invited Agnes to one of the afternoon parties that he and his wife gave in the Kensington house they rented for the London season. At the same time he undertook to write again to the *Free Review* to 'wake them up' if the following week brought no news.

This proved to be unnecessary and Hardy was able to write to Agnes to congratulate her on the acceptance of her article, which was to appear in the July issue. It is noteworthy that the editor dealt personally with Hardy, sending him the letter of acceptance and subsequently the proofs for correction. On June 21 Agnes noted curtly in her diary 'Received *Free Review*. Signature wrong'. The article was credited to 'Mrs. Walter Grove', whereas she had wanted her own signature.

With due allowance for changing customs and standards it is fair to claim that 'What children should be told' was a challenging and radical piece of journalism, which justified Hardy's comment that – by virtue of its sincerity and honesty – it should win the respect of those even who were most opposed to the views it expressed. She must have touched a raw nerve in many young parents like herself when she asked 'Why should it be considered wise or expedient that the young are to be taught to reverence a Church by those who have ceased to do so themselves?'. She aligned herself openly with those 'who have left the stereotyped paths of the religion in which they were brought up' and found 'an endless source of inspiriting hope in the teachings of such modern thinkers as Mill, Spencer, Huxley, Kant and Fichte'.

Her comments on sex education are couched in the awkward and blurring delicacies of language that were more or less obligatory at the time, but the trend of her thinking is clear enough. She criticised particularly the women who allowed their sons to believe their mothers 'ignorant of certain sins' – a false modesty which prevented such women from imparting 'the fruits of their experience and the knowledge brought by their years'. What Agnes sought to define was the proper and distinct demarcation between reticence and falsehood.

Encouraged by this first success she applied her pen to other topics, sending her drafts to Hardy for comment and guidance. Her industry impressed him. 'What an energetic scribe you are becoming!' he wrote. When he received her greetings on New Year's Day, 1897, he replied with an approving schoolmasterly report on her work in the previous year. 'Upon the whole', he wrote, 'you may congratulate yourself upon your advance during the year past: you have obtained a firmer hold upon the pen, and are in a fair way of being well known as a writer'. To Mrs. Henniker he wrote at this time 'Agnes Grove has another article about to appear – did she tell you?' He knew that Agnes had been to Mrs. Henniker's party just before Christmas and he seemed to take a pleasure in the closer association of his two pupils.

Chapter Fourteen

Agnes's friendship with Thomas Hardy was part of a general widening of her social circle in the later nineties. Another important influence was that of Sybil, Lady Queensberry, whose periods of residence at Hatch, near Tisbury, made her a country neighbour of Agnes's. Having in common an interest in amateur theatricals and in the arts generally the two women became close friends. Lady Queensberry, who was an artist of some accomplishment, sculpted a bust of Agnes; and her daughter, Edith Douglas, married Agnes's brother, St. George, in 1898.

The shared theatrical endeavour at Hatch was nothing if not ambitious. In the summer of 1896 Mrs. Patrick Campbell was persuaded to take part and two professional actors, Mr. Fosse and Mr. Barker, arrived a week ahead of her to join the rehearsals. Mrs. Pat contented herself with a single dress rehearsal on the day before the performance, which 'went off really extremely well', in Agnes's estimation. Characteristically Agnes added, 'My song was much liked'.

The friendship that developed with Mrs. Patrick Campbell emphasised the easy mingling of stage personalities with the conventional aristocracy during the nineties. A month before the theatricals at Hatch Agnes had attended the wedding of Lady Jeune's daughter, Dorothy, to Henry Allhusen, who became member of Parliament for Salisbury in the following year. Mingling with the guests, who included Anthony Hope and Thomas Hardy, Agnes noted 'much family' and also 'G. Alexander the actor, Grossmith etc.'

Between the Allhusen wedding and the Hatch theatricals Agnes went to Bayreuth. She was an enthusiastic Wagnerite, heard the complete *Ring* cycle twice and went to Madame Wagner's party: after which she returned to London 'without incident beyond Giovanni the footman being left behind'. Two years later she renewed her pleasure in Wagner's operas at Covent Garden: the brief diary entries are worth quoting –

> June 27. In the evening Flo Henniker, Duke of Abercorn and Mr. Walker came to Rheingold in box lent me by [illegible]. Walter took Grace Heathcott who dined with us.
>
> June 29. Went to opera, Walkure.
>
> June 30. Went to Siegfried. Rushed home to dress. Went after the opera to supper at the Savoy with Mrs. P. Campbell, Sarah Bernhardt, the Trees, Forbes Robertson, Mrs. Schuster, Mr. George Wyndham. Sarah Bernhardt delightful.

The friendship with Mrs. Pat was genuine and enduring. Frequent entries in Agnes's diary show the two women together, lunching at the Garrick Club, or dining at the Café Royal with Forbes Robertson after *Hamlet*. The actress took Agnes 'behind the scenes' when she was playing in *Magda*, and Agnes entertained Mrs. Pat and her two children to tea. As late as 1918, more than twenty years after their first meeting, Agnes recorded 'Luncheon with Mrs. Pat Campbell and Stella, her daughter.'

At the same time Agnes was making a place for herself in the new political world of post-Gladstone Liberalism. In the spring of 1896 she and Walter went with Sir Thomas to join a house-party near Trowbridge where their fellow guests included the Asquiths. A month later, in London, she took Lady Queensberry's daughter to a party given by the Asquiths, where she also found incidentally the now familiar figure of Thomas Hardy, with his wife Emma.

The Asquith party was evidently a prelude to a Liberal conference. Four days later her diary reads 'My speech day. Was very nervous. Went to Council meeting about 11. My speech came on in afternoon. Success!' Next day she had luncheon with the Asquiths after a Council meeting, and on the following day the scene changed to a literary tea party at the Hardys. *The Life of Thomas Hardy* describes these occasions as 'a form then in vogue, one very convenient for literary persons, of having afternoon parties'. At the apartment he rented in South Kensington for the London season he and Emma gave a number of such parties, 'doing as much themselves to entertain people as they could accomplish in a house not their own'. Agnes's diary shows the kind of people one might expect to meet there. On this particular occasion she noted the Henry Normans; the poet and novelist Hamilton Aidé who was an old friend of one of Hardy's architect-employers, Sir Arthur Blomfield; the sculptor, Hamo Thornycroft; Florence Henniker and her sister, Lady Fitz-gerald; Lady Wynford; and the young poet, Lionel Johnson, who had recently published *The Art of Thomas Hardy*, the first of what was destined to become an avalanche of critical studies.

With her literary and political interests, and her aristocratic background, Agnes was enviably rich in the range of her acquaintances. In the closing years of the century she had many agreeable and interesting events to record in her diary: meeting Rudyard Kipling with his wife in the Larmer Tree Gardens; staying with the Hennikers at Eton and with Lord Crewe at Fryston; going on board the Royal Yacht at Cowes; meeting fashionable writers of the time – Olive Schreiner, Pearl Craigie ('John Oliver Hobbes'), Alfred Austin and others – wintering at Mentone, theatre-going in London and theatrical suppers afterwards with the leading players; moments of success as a public speaker on her chosen subjects of Liberalism, anti-vivisection and women's suffrage; and the publication of more of her essays which drew from Hardy his congratulation on her 'steady advance as a writer and thinker.'

There was, however, a darker side to these sunlit years. The foundations of Agnes's world were not in London but in the obscure countryside of Tollard Royal and the Donheads and Berwick St. John. She was daughter and wife in two great landowning families, at Rushmore and at Ferne. The twin pillars of that world were the two fathers, Sir Thomas and the General, seemingly unshakeable but – like other men in this if in nothing else – fallible and mortal.

In 1896 Sir Thomas entered into a discreet correspondence about two portraits by Romney, which hung at Ferne. One was of Mrs. Thomas Grove of Ferne, Sir Thomas's grandmother who was also an aunt of the poet Shelley. The other was of Elizabeth Grove of Ferne, grandfather Thomas's sister, who married her cousin William Chafyn Grove MP of Zeals. The purpose of Sir Thomas's correspondence, with Vicars Brothers of Old Bond Street, was to commission an artist to paint replicas to hang in place of the originals, which would thereupon be acquired by Vicars Brothers in return for a cash payment of £2900.

The price seemed attractive at the time but became less so after a thoughtful conversation with another dealer, Wertheimer. Sir Thomas, well able to recognise the difference between £2900 and £3500, decided to terminate his deal with Vicars and close with Wertheimer. His diary records a tense moment when representatives of the two dealers called at Ferne on the same day, but fortunately at different times and did not meet. Eventually Vicars threatened legal action to enforce their agreement and the story ended with the laconic entry 'The pictures came from Vicars' and next day 'The pictures were hung in the dining-room'. The Romneys departed.

This little episode finds its place here as a straw in a wind that was blowing increasingly chill. In the public eye Sir Thomas must have seemed a secure and wealthy man, owner of a great mansion, farming or renting to his tenants thousands of acres as ten generations of Groves had done before him. But the final decades of the nineteenth century were an unkind climate for landowners of his sort. British agriculture was drifting into the long years of depression and stagnation, which were only temporarily checked by the siege conditions of the 1914 War. The great estates felt increasing pressures, which many were unable to resist. While wages were rising, tenancy rents went unpaid or had to be reduced. At the half-yearly Rent Audit at Ferne in 1889 nearly half the rents were unpaid although the amounts seem not to have risen significantly from those ruling forty years earlier.

It is not possible from the papers that survive to analyse completely the financial problems that beset Sir Thomas, but his diaries give some indication of the growing menace that prompted the sale of the Romneys. These diaries, incidentally, are characteristic of the man. Each year, from 1855 to 1897 he bought an identical copy of 'The Gentleman's Pocket Diary'. On the right-hand pages he entered items of payments made, on the left a brief account of each day's events – predominantly hunting conditions and shooting bags – with occasional notes of a payment received. Most Sundays he attended church, most weekdays he shot or hunted when he was not in Parliament, sailing at Weymouth, or training with the Yeomanry. Somewhat surprisingly, perhaps, he was a keen opera-goer.

His inheritance of Ferne in 1858 was certainly a rich one: his mother had added a dowry of £10,000 to the already considerable wealth of the Groves, which included properties in Norfolk and

Cornwall as well as the main estates in Wiltshire. In about 1861 Thomas felt able to add a further two thousand or more acres at Winterslow, near Salisbury, for which he paid 50,000 guineas. His election to Parliament in 1865 and his subsequent baronetcy mark the high tidemark of his career. However, his initial election expenses had exceeded £5000 and by 1873 his net income was seemingly £2000 short of his annual expenditure. Against this background his attitude in 1882 to Walter's choice of Agnes as the future baronet's wife is more readily understandable. In Sir Thomas's view the moment had come for an heiress to bring a fresh dowry of sufficient weight to restore the Grove fortunes. Walter's comment at the time, that his father 'thinks a man an egregious ass who marries for anything but money, and looks upon being in love with a woman like a slight cold in the head' was no more than the plain truth. Sir Thomas's diary reveals that his own search for a widow suitably endowed to become the second Lady Grove was conducted on just such lines. Once a quarter he noted in his diary a payment from Lady Grove which added up to £1500 a year. And when Frances gave birth to their first and only child, Olivia, he recorded 'She to pay me £100 per annum for her cost from Jan 1st.'

Nevertheless, the danger signals were already plain to see in 1893 when he sold the Cornish property – presumably to keep his creditors at bay, as he was still chronically short of cash. A quarterly allowance of £25 to one of his daughters was paid by £5 in cash accompanied by a cheque of Lady Grove's for £20: six months later his private account was overdrawn by £3000 and the bank was becoming restive. In December 1894 his payment of interest on a £25,000 mortgage was so overdue that he was threatened with drastic action unless he paid by return of post. Visits with his wife to the bank in Shaftesbury continue the story. 'Called at bank. Renewed bill with Frances', is one diary entry at this time, and another reads 'Frances and self signed promissory note'. At the same time he was compelled to allow reductions in rent, to offset the agricultural depression.

It was a worried and financially imperilled man, therefore, who in the autumn of 1896 surveyed the fake Romneys newly hung in his dining room at Ferne. The very next day brought another picture to hang with them, a portrait of Mr. Gladstone offered to Sir Thomas by a Mr. Stewart. Sir Thomas accepted it, with such thoughts as one can only guess at. To Gladstone he owed his baronetcy. The

Grand Old Man was the leader he had admired and followed – but finally had deserted. When Gladstone's Irish policy was rejected by Parliament, after a split in his own party, Sir Thomas's was one of the votes cast with the opposition. It was an act for which many of his constituency supporters never forgave him. A formal letter from the South Wilts Central Liberal Association thanking Sir Thomas for his great services up to the time when Gladstone introduced his Irish Home Rule bill, but regretting his political action subsequently, was a plain enough indication that his parliamentary career was crumbling. When he next had to face re-election he was defeated and did not stand again.

A month after the hanging of the pictures the Ferne dining-room was the scene of a pleasant Christmas party when Walter and Agnes brought their children to dine with Sir Thomas and Frances and their daughter, Olivia, now twelve years old. Agnes and her family usually spent Christmas Day at Ferne, and she and Sir Thomas seem to have settled into a mutual esteem in spite of the fact that almost his last action as a member of Paliament was to vote against women's suffrage. He took an interest in Agnes's local campaigning, attending one of her suffrage meetings in Easton barn at Berwick and making a speech there.

That Christmas party of 1896 was to be the last such occasion. Three weeks later, while visiting a married daughter, Sir Thomas died suddenly. Walter succeeded to the baronetcy and to what could be salvaged of the ancestral estate. Agnes became Lady Grove. The visitors' book at Ferne closed on April 3, 1897 with a final entry 'Mabel Bond, Olivia Frances Grove, Charlotte A. Grove, Frances Hinton Grove left Ferne. Finis.'

Meanwhile at Rushmore the General's health was failing although his unremitting application to his archaeological work showed as yet no sign of slackening. In 1897 he was completing the fourth volume of his *Excavations in Cranborne Chase* for publication the following year; and also supervising, at Iwerne, what was to be his last excavation. In this period Agnes had little contact with him and was sadly unappreciative of the importance of his investigations of prehistory. On one occasion she took her two elder children to see a 'dig' at Sixpenny Handley where they were shown two skeletons 'side by side without heads', but she did not enjoy seeing money spent on such a pursuit. There was a great scene of reconciliation with Papa in 1894 but not much further contact until she realised that he was seriously ill. In August 1899 she wrote in her diary 'P very ill', adding the characteristic comment 'at loggerheads with the nurse'. His life was ending with the century. In the following May he died: Agnes, going to Rushmore to pay her last respects to 'the Man', was struck by his beauty as he lay at peace.

With the deaths of Sir Thomas and the General the two great houses of Ferne and Rushmore passed into untried and weaker hands. Rushmore was to retain its character as her family home during the rest of Agnes's lifetime, but Ferne was already doomed. Within the year the house itself was let to Lord James of Hereford and Walter put the farm stock and equipment up for sale. Sir Thomas had farmed directly about 2000 acres. Into the sale now went his breeding flock of over 800 Hampshire Down ewes and lambs, with 90 cattle and 15 horses to swell the total to exceed £2500. A year later Walter sold some minor properties, including *The Grove Arms* at Ludwell and another *Grove Arms* at Berwick St. John. It was the beginning of a long and inexorable retreat.

During the arguments about Agnes's marriage settlement Sir Thomas had laid great emphasis on the reliable security of his will to safeguard Walter's position. His death disclosed that he had made no will. This did at least justify the General's much resented insistence at the time that an income for Agnes, if she survived Walter, should be secured on land designated for the purpose. However Sir Thomas had suffered a lapse of memory at some later date when he mortgaged the land without recalling the restriction placed on it.

In all the circumstances of his intestacy Sir Thomas's widow behaved with magnanimity. Waiving her rights she desired Walter to be authorised as sole executor. Mourning the loss now of her third husband she settled in Maperton and exchanged occasional visits with Agnes and Walter. When the children of Sir Thomas's first marriage erected an imposing memorial plaque in Berwick St. John church Frances placed separately an unobtrusive brass tablet from herself and Olivia.

For Agnes one immediate consequence of Sir Thomas's death was a move, not to Ferne – as might have been expected – but to the manor house at Sedgehill. This was another Grove property, on an altogether smaller scale than Ferne but a very pleasing and suitable 'seat' for the new baronet and his family. It was with evident satisfaction that Agnes printed in capital letters in her diary the words 'LEFT BERWICK FOR GOOD'.

Sedgehill is some three or four miles north of Shaftesbury and its Grove connection dates back to Elizabethan times when Robert Grove, a Shaftesbury lawyer, made good use of his employment by Lord Arundell and Lord Pembroke to become a man of property in his own right and to gain a coat of arms. Sedgehill was one of his acquisitions, along with Ferne and Stoke Trister. In more recent times one of Sir Thomas's uncles had been rector of Sedgehill, while another uncle had farmed there. The manor house itself had a romantic literary association that should have appealed to Agnes: in 1811 it was the bridal home of Harriet Grove after she broke off her engagement to her cousin, the poet Shelley, and instead married William Helyar. By a strange coincidence Harriet christened one of her children Agnes Grove Helyar.

The house saw surprisingly little of Agnes and Walter in the first years of their occupancy. Agnes liked to be in London for the Season and to go abroad in the winter. Walter seemed to be drawn closer to his brother, Tom, and his two younger sisters, Charlotte and Kate. Tom had left England as a young man to try his luck in the New World, at first in the Argentine and subsequently in California with one of his Bruce cousins. In 1899 Walter decided to take Charlotte with him on a vist to Tom in California – a visit that was to have important consequences in later years.

Kate and her soldier-husband, Eddy Pleydell, had been out of touch with Agnes and Walter while Eddy was serving in India, but the old comradeship revived after Sir Thomas's death. There was talk between them of the attractions of North Africa as a winter resort increasingly favoured by the English. The year after he had taken Charlotte to California, Walter was ready to join forces with sister Kate and her husband. And Agnes was certainly not averse to an adventurous journey during which she found the material for her first book.

She was by now a recognised contributor of controversial essays to several periodicals, particularly on social topics and women's suffrage. Hardy continued to supervise and encourage her efforts. One of her suffrage articles drew from him the comment 'I don't know any woman writer who puts such vigour into her sentences as you do, or who is so dexterous in the conduct of an argument of that kind, and this power of yours makes me feel that you should give your attention exclusively to essay writing, and not to fiction, and also makes me proud of you as a pupil.' In a postscript he added 'Em is enthusiastic about the article and agrees with every word.'

Emma's recognition of Agnes as an ally in the campaign for women's rights must have eased the relationship between the two women and made Agnes a welcome visitor to Max Gate. In February 1900 Agnes drove with Ivor Guest to Dorchester to see Hardy, and a month later she stayed the night at Max Gate. Emma met her at the station and after a pleasant dinner Agnes had a long talk with Hardy.

In the following September two of Agnes's essays, later collected in *The Human Woman*, were translated to be presented as a paper in Paris where she attended the *Congrès International de la Condition et des Droits des Femmes.* And in December she and her family sailed from Liverpool in the *Britannia* to Tangier, where they joined forces with the Pleydells.

Chapter Fifteen

In 1902 Longmans Green & Co. published *Seventy-one Days' Camping in Morocco* by Lady Grove, with photogravure portrait and 32 illustrations from photographs. It was her first book and it was well received by the Press. She described her arrival in Tangier during 'the last month of the last century' when her intention was simply to spend the 'winter abroad in the ordinary conventional way'. Her eldest daughter, Honor, was approaching her eighteenth birthday and the appropriate moment to be presented at Court as a *débutante*. The family would therefore return to London for the Season. Meanwhile they planned to enjoy the social life of the English colony in the vicinity of Tangier. Walter was scarcely off the boat before he was away with his sister Kate Pleydell and her husband on a pig-sticking expedition; and Agnes soon joined in.

Allowing for a new set of names her diary entries are much as they might have been in England. There is the familiar round of luncheon, tea and dinner parties, the paying of social calls and leaving of cards, the general restlessness in pursuit of novelty and pleasure. Not all the names are unfamiliar. A Russell appears among the diplomats – Claud Russell, who seems to have captivated Agnes immediately. On a pig-sticking sortie she 'rode with Mr. Russell part of the time and found him pleasant'. Three days later he came to tea and when she saw him off on his departure next day she confessed to being 'quite sad'. A day later she went into the town and an enigmatic note records that she 'found a telegram which interested me'. It may not have been from Claud Russell, but later events support the possibility.

Another familiar name was that of R.B. Cunninghame Graham, whose mother and brother, Charles, Agnes had certainly known in London, so she was probably not meeting Robert for the first time when they found themselves in each other's company in Tangier. His book, *Mogreb-el-Acksa: a journey in Morocco*, had been published in 1898, and he visited the country frequently in subsequent years.

It was an event on January 23, 1901, that disturbed Agnes's plans. A rumour spread that Queen Victoria had died the previous evening. A call at the British Legation confirmed the news. In England the Court was in mourning and would remain so. The forthcoming Season was extinguished and so therefore was the reason for returning. In Agnes's words 'An event of grave, national, world-wide importance contributed chiefly towards our decision to stay in Morocco; and the daughter for whose sake we would have returned home made her first functional curtsey in the presence of Royalty to the Sultan of Morocco, instead of to the Queen of England.'

Their wanderings took them into the Atlas mountains, where they tried to hunt mouflon, and as far from Tangier as Marrakesh and Mogador. On the main expedition, when they were living under canvas in arduous circumstances, their younger children were left behind in the care of governesses and servants. Sometimes they stayed in hotels, at other times at a house Agnes had rented in the mountains. The squalor and discomfort of some of their camping sites contrasted with the luxurious parties in Tangier. Walter, who was keeping a diary spasmodically at this time, described a dance given by the Russian Minister as 'a very pretty ball: most of the people went in Fancy Dress or *poudré*. There was a cotillion and it was well done'. Agnes looked very well 'with her hair powdered and in a white draped gown as a Sir Joshua Reynolds picture'.

Most of 1901 was spent in Morocco although Walter returned to England briefly in March, probably in connection with the intended sale of Ferne. Lord James's tenancy had ended, and the house was to be auctioned on July 30. Walter and Agnes were both in England at that time, though neither recorded what happened at the auction. The house remained unsold, presumably having failed to achieve its reserve price. It was therefore leased to a London merchant, Mr. Schwann, until February 3, 1902 for thirty guineas a week, his purpose being to enjoy the sporting rights. Having failed to sell Ferne, Walter parted with some land at Sedgehill in October 1901;

and on the 25th of that month Agnes sailed to Gibralter and Tangier, having heard that her book was accepted by Longmans for publication.

Their second winter in Morocco was passed in much the same way as the first. Boar hunts, fancy dress balls, polo matches and children's parties made up the social calendar. Even so, Agnes did not neglect her writing. 'Wrote hard all day and sent off article to Cornhill', she noted in her diary. Walter's love of field sports took a new turn when he teamed up with Meade Waldo, who was collecting specimens of rare birds for the British Museum of Natural History and had with him a man named Vauché, who served a dual purpose as interpreter and taxidermist. The three men sailed from Tangier to Casablanca, with the intention of shooting specimens of great bustard in the Forest of Marmora, which it was thought were a different species from those near Tangier. The eggs of the Abyssinian rock ibis, nesting on the cliffs near Talli, were also to be collected and sent to London. Walter's particular interest was to see the country inland of Rabat where, he wrote, 'The tribes are under no sort of government and the sultan himself cannot go through the district and has to go round when he travels from Marrakesh to Fez'.

The pursuit of the great bustard evidently needed more time than Walter had arranged to give it. Too long was spent in negotiating the hire of mules and getting the expedition started. It took them four days to reach the Forest of Marmora, of which Walter gives this description –

> The Forest extends for three day's march and is a perfect paradise for the sportsman. The naturalist Meade Waldo got a great spotted cuckoo and several new butterflies, hitherto unknown to entomologists, and we saw any amount of rare birds. The flowers are quite lovely, the whole place one mass of colour.
>
> We had a very long walk in the Forest, beating it for bustard. We saw several, but did not get a shot. They all got up out of shot. It is hopeless to shoot at them if they are more than 25 yards off, and as we are always accompanied by a lot of wild arabs who talk at the top of their voices and whistle and gesticulate all the time the chances of getting near them are extremely remote.

> We were much disappointed as this particular bustard has never been identified. It is known not to be the same as the European bird. Its habits and call are different and the Natural History Museum is very anxious to get a specimen.

As a consolation prize Walter shot a bald-headed Abyssinian Ibis, which Vauché skinned, and then the journey back to Tangier began. Shortly after his arrival Walter went to the pier with Agnes to see Honor aboard a ship bound for England, accompanied by the British ambassador's wife and doubtless prepared to make her curtsey to Queen Alexandra in the new season. On May 1st Walter himself decided to return for a fresh attempt to sell Ferne, leaving Agnes with the younger children in Tangier.

This time the house found a buyer, the Duke of Hamilton. As it has since been demolished it merits a brief description here. It stood in 300 acres of woodland with an inner park of 13 acres approached by two carriage drives. Besides the two lodges there were coachman's, groom's and keeper's houses. The mansion had been built during the years 1809-1811 on the site of an earlier building. The entrance hall led to a large inner hall, open to the second floor, with a marble gallery and columns. There were six bedrooms on the first floor, eleven on the second which also had space for a full-size billiards table. A separate wing contained four large bedrooms for maidservants and three for men (with their own staircase). In its heyday up to two hundred guests had danced at a Ferne ball, three thousand had attended its garden fêtes. If offered 500 acres of coverts and rabbit warrens to the sportsman, with an estimated annual game bag of a thousand partridges and seven thousand rabbits. Sixteen farms and numerous smallholdings, belonging to the estate, brought in a net income of about £3000. Tithes were paid in four parishes, Berwick St. John, Donhead St. Mary, Donhead St. Andrew and Tollard Royal.

The best of the family silver – mostly of the William & Mary or Queen Anne periods – went to a London auction room. Three centuries of solid and prosperous worth were declining to a precipitate conclusion. The mortgages and loans were paid off. An income remained, on which Walter and Agnes evidently believed they could maintain something like the standard of life they had now adopted. The grandeur of the past had gone but the new century in its Edwardian style looked promising. In the week before Whitsun

Walter sent a telegram to Tangier giving Agnes the news that represented the end of an anxious time – 'Ferne all sold'.

The telegram was not handed to her until the morning of the following day – a day that was to persist in her memory for a very different reason. The three children, Gerald, Oenone and Terence, came to her to hear the news from their father and she then sent them to play in the garden. The Russian Minister had invited her to lunch. Gerald was supposed to go to the stable to have Agnes's horse made ready for her to ride. At first he forgot: when he went eventually, Oenone followed him. Terence was left alone.

Agnes rode away to her appointment but had scarcely arrived when a telephone message recalled her. There had been an accident. She galloped back to find that Terence had fallen into a pool and drowned. He was eight years old, her youngest and perhaps her favourite child.

Her grief was violent and theatrical. She wrote and published privately a strange allegory, *How Time began to Count*, in which Terence becomes a sort of Peter Pan figure. She had a large mural of Terence and herself, based on a photograph, painted on the chimney breast above the fireplace at Sedgehill. And of course the Moroccan adventure was over. What had been on its way to becoming a second home was now but an evil and haunting memory.

After the first stunning blow of bereavement Agnes's diary gives little impression of the passing of the remainder of the year. In the autumn she and Walter spent a few days near Wiesbaden with Sybil Queensberry. The midwinter went unrecorded, probably at Sedgehill. When she resumed her diary at the end of January 1903 she was riding to hounds with Walter and entertaining friends or visiting Frances in Sherborne, where Gerald was now at school and Oenone was about to enter the new school for girls that opened there in March. Thomas Hardy and Emma were among the guests expected at Sedgehill at this time. In a letter to Florence Henniker in March Hardy said he had been disabled by a protracted attack of rheumatism, and added 'We were going to stay for a day or two with Lady Grove at Sedgehill, but had to put off on two occasions on account of it.'

To Agnes Hardy wrote regretfully 'there is nobody I should more like to visit than yourself, as I am sure you know, or if you don't you ought to guess it;' and he went on to ask 'What are you doing in the literary way?'. Her long absences in Morocco had interrupted the earlier pattern of meetings and correspondence, and of Hardy's close supervision of her writing. As she re-established her life in England, and put the shock of Terence's death behind her, it was a case of taking up the threads again – though with a difference.

Sedgehill was small beer after Rushmore and Ferne. The brothers and sisters who had meant so much to Agnes and Walter twenty years ago were scattered now. Kate and Eddy Pleydell stayed on in Morocco until 1914. Charlotte married in 1904 but the event went unrecorded in Agnes's diary. St. George and Lionel appeared from time to time, and there was still an occasional visit to Walter's married sister at Clewer, but the intense intimacies of that tightly knit world of their youth had gone. Agnes was forty in 1903 and Edwardian London was a new scene that beckoned to her. She could reasonably think of herself now as a professional writer, and she cannot have been indifferent to a source of additional income. Her occasional essays found a ready enough market and in November 1903 she noted 'Went city by train for interview Fleet St. 12.30 with Editor and Managing Director of New Magazine. Had long interview'. A fortnight later the editor offered her ten guineas a month as a regular contributor. When Hardy heard of this he wrote to her,

> Your leap into journalism is startling to sober minds like mine. But I see no reason why you should not get along swimmingly, as you have passed your apprenticeship, and are by nature courageous. I hope I may see you soon, but not *looking* like a journalist; merely as you used to look will satisfy me.

Perhaps more surprisingly, Walter also was embarking on a career which held out a prospect of financial benefit. In the summer of 1903 T.W. Barber's Inventions Ltd. issued a prospectus for thirty thousand £1 shares, with Walter as one of the company's five directors. The inventions of the ingenious Mr. Barber included variable-speed gears, a friction clutch and a steam motor car. So compelling is the confidence radiated by the prospectus that one is dismayed to find no shred of evidence of Walter's further progress as a company director. Agnes's diaries shed no light on the enterprise, though it must be admitted that they are a very incomplete record of this period and Walter's role in them is a shadowy one.

In the spring of 1904 Agnes gave birth to a son. He must have seemed a consolation and a replacement for the tragically lost

Terence. Instinctively Agnes named him Walter but when he was christened at Westminster Abbey, with Sybil Queensberry as one of his godmothers, his full name was given as Walter Peel Grove. The choice of 'Peel' is a puzzling and teasing one, because it seems to have no family association and it therefore points to a character frequently mentioned by Agnes at this time – Willy Peel. His presence is first noticeable in Agnes's diary as 'W. Peel' in the spring of 1903. He gradually becomes identifiable as William Robert Wellesley Peel (1867-1937) who succeeded as Viscount Peel in 1912 and became Earl Peel in 1929. Three months after the christening he took Agnes to a ball at Buckingham Palace, and one might assume that he was a godfather to the infant Walter Peel. That would account for the choice of his name, but it was not the case. The godfathers were Agnes's brother, Lionel, and a Dutch friend from their Moroccan days, Baron van Heemstra who married a niece of Walter's.

The most one can say of Willy Peel's place in Agnes's life is that he is one of the three men who at this time fulfilled the roles occupied twenty years earlier by Dawson-Damer and Chandos Pole. They were her courtiers and her squires in a sort of wry charade that lay somewhere between flirtation and friendship. The other two were Henry Guest and Claud Russell.

Just as Claud Russell had appealed instantly to Agnes at their first meeting in Morocco, so did Captain Guest in the spring of 1903 when he arrived as a guest at Freethorpe near Norwich where Agnes had joined the house-party three days earlier. A Captain Fraser was also a guest and had not found favour with Agnes. As the week ended she made one of her characteristically dramatic entries in her diary – 'Then Captain Guest arrived. I liked him at once. Had embroglio with Captain Fraser'.

It rained all next day. On the following day her diary reads – 'Drove to Haviland with Captain Guest and played chess (?) with him in the evening. Was almost happy'. The question mark after 'chess' is hers. Next morning Captain Guest accompanied her on the train to London, where she was due to meet Walter, dine with friends and go to a theatre. A more impromptu engagement ends the day: 'then Captain Guest came to supper with us'. He met Agnes again next morning at the zoo and joined her at lunch with Willy Peel. He also called on the following morning to see Agnes before she returned to Sedgehill, where he was invited to visit for a golf match with Mr. Grosvenor. Two of the children inconveniently developed mumps at this moment, causing Mr. Grosvenor to stay away and postponing Captain Guest's arrival. However, within a week the captain was installed at Sedgehill and taking Agnes for a daily drive to Canford or Wardour. When Agnes returned to London she went to the opera with Willy Peel and lunched with him next day, but then 'telephoned to Guest who came about 6 to see me'. The following afternoon she went to Windsor, 'motored with Capt Guest, dined with him and returned about 10.30.'

That was on May 17, just three weeks after their first meeting at the house-party in Norfolk. Regrettably Agnes lost interest in her diary at this moment. Apart from a brief spell in November she had virtually nothing she wanted to record in its pages and they remain tantalisingly blank. Captain Guest is lost to view, disappearing as suddenly as he entered. His christian name is never given in the diary but Agnes preserved a photo of 'Henry Guest in motor', which presumably identifies him.

The diaries come to life again in the winter of 1903/4 when Agnes, Walter and the children spent some weeks in Paris. Back in London in the spring Agnes was confined with Walter Peel; after the birth of her baby she looked for a settled London address and chose 51 Bedford Square as her future *salon*. Her diary entries were erratic in the summer but in July Willy Peel was evidently having to compete with Claud Russell for Agnes's interest. As a young diplomat Russell's postings abroad may have given him no opportunity to develop the promise of that first meeting in Morocco at Easter in 1901. Be that as it may, he lost no time in the summer of 1904. Day after day he came to luncheon or tea, and sometimes to both. An entry in August shows Agnes in the centre of her chosen circle of men –

> I left Semley by 1 o'clock train, arrived London 3. Mr. Herbert, St. George, Willy Peel and Claud Russell came to tea. St. G. and Claud R dined. W.P. came after. We met in the Square. C.R. stayed on. Delightful evening.

Her diaries no longer received the passionate confidences that enriched the early years and now tended increasingly to chronicle the barest outline of events, but there are moments in her relationship with Russell when the strength of her feelings is felt. At the end of 1904 their frequent meetings had to end when he was posted to the embassy staff in Paris. In the following spring, after a holiday with Walter on the Franco-Spanish border, she left Walter at Bordeaux and spent four days with Claud in Paris, dining at the Ritz and being generally entertained by him. When it was time to part he accompanied her to Boulogne.

Next winter she went to Switzerland with Walter, Oenone and the infant Walter who had by now acquired the nickname 'Beb', by which he was to be known in future. Agnes's health seems to have been the motive for the journey; she took her temperature daily and consulted a doctor who pronounced her as certainly suffering from tuberculosis. Walter returned to England after a while and Agnes sent messages to Willy Peel and Claud Russell who responded with sympathetic telegrams promising to join her. Peel was the first to arrive and stayed for five days, after which Agnes and the children moved on to Milan and Alassio. It was Easter when Claud arrived 'looking very thin and with a cold'.

The visit was not a success. When Claud left after five days he dutifully sent a telegram from Paris to say he had 'enjoyed the visit!' Agnes noted the words with a sardonic and ominous exclamation mark. A letter from Claud followed and as soon as Agnes was back in London a month later he 'came to see me early in the morning and we had an agreeable reconciliation'. It was a pattern of events in which she was well versed. The suddenly gathering storm and the later relaxations of mutual forgiveness provide a familiar graph of Agnes's emotions.

Chapter Sixteen

On February 9, 1905 Agnes committed to her diary this enigmatic entry – 'Frank came to luncheon. We went together to Bow Street where they made me pay 26/- costs. But I had my say.'

'Frank' was perhaps the elder brother of Bertrand Russell and accompanied Agnes to the magistrate's court as her legal adviser and to give her moral support. But what crime had she committed? Was it some act of suffragette militancy? On what theme did she 'have her say' before paying the twenty-six shillings?.

The explanation is an anticlimax that borders on the ludicrous. She had not had Beb vaccinated. Moreover her change of address from Kensington to Bedford Square had so delayed the delivery of the official form that the time in which she could register a conscientious objection had expired. Her argument that a scruple of conscience, judged to be valid at three months after the birth of the child, was no less authentic a scruple at ten months must appear to be logically irrefutable; but the magistrate took the view that the law is the law, and logic does not enter into it.

The incident is mentioned here only because it establishes a useful fact in a period which is poorly documented. After the return from Morocco Agnes entered increasingly into London life and was soon active as a hostess, but seems not to have had a settled establishment in London. Her diaries suggest that she sometimes spent a night or two in a hotel, sometimes stayed with her sister, Alice Lubbock, or with Sybil Queensberry; and at other times she probably rented a house or an apartment for the season, as was the custom. But by 1905 she was installed at Bedford Square and, in default of any contrary evidence, one may assume that this was her *salon* and her London headquarters during the Edwardian years which marked the peak of her literary career. Her diary for 1907 has very few entries and those for 1908 to 1914 are either lost or never existed. To reconstruct the period one must rely on correspondence – hers and other people's – and on miscellaneous items that have survived. She had visiting cards printed for herself and Honor bearing the address 51 Bedford Square, and it also appears on the pasteboard programme of a musical *soirée* that she gave. She was using the address in 1909 but probably no later than that.

During the years 1906-10 she was active in journalism and published three books. Her circle of acquaintance had an increasingly literary flavour. In her haste she sometimes provides no more clue than 'people came to luncheon' but when the names of guests are given one notices Max Beerbohm, Hilaire Belloc, Alice Meynell, Logan Pearsall Smith, Horace Vachell and Robert Cunninghame Graham. Belloc wrote her lively and amusing letters, Graham assured her earnestly that 'Morris is a true poet, and does by nature what Yeats strives to do by culture'.

Supremely of course there was the friendship with Hardy. On successive days in May 1906 Agnes and Sybil Queensberry went to tea with the Hardys, and Hardy returned the visit next day. Writing of these tea-parties at about this time Jacques-Emile Blanche, the portrait painter, in his book of reminiscences *Mes Modèles* gives the impression that Agnes acted as Hardy's hostess, even when Emma was present – 'C'est lady Grove qui semblait recevoir, lors de petites *tea-parties* où nous fûmes convoqués, au flat meublé du cher ménage provincial. Mrs. Hardy la laissait minauder avec les plumitifs.'

Blanche is certainly not a witness whose testimony deserves to be accepted unreservedly. Emma was in her middle sixties and by 1908 was feeling too weak to undertake the task of housekeeping in a London house as well as at Max Gate. She may not have been entirely reluctant a year or two earlier, therefore, to let a younger woman lend a hand with some of the duties of entertaining 'les plumitifs' who crowded round Hardy. Blanche may or may not interpret Emma's feeling accurately but he does establish that Agnes was a regular and intimate member of the Hardys' circle of friends in London at this time.

It is clear too that Hardy had resumed his practical interest in Agnes's progress as a writer. The book on which she embarked in

1906, and which was published in 1907, bears the dedication 'To Thomas Hardy in grateful recognition of timely aid and counsel, and in memory of old and enduring friendship'. He had read the book in the 'proof' stage, making corrections and suggestions as he had done with her earlier essays in the nineties. She was once again the good little pupil.

The title of her book was *The Social Fetich*, which she interpreted in her preface thus –

> A due respect for the good governance of society is as wholesome as an undue insistence upon its temporarily established customs is mischievous and shortsighted.
>
> Like all laws, social laws are only made for those likely to break them. To be a slave to convention is to be doubtful of one's own security. The worship of convention is a fetich as hydra-headed and as disintegrating, both to the individual and the community, as any other sinister idolatry.
>
> In the essays that follow I have tried lightly to sketch the composition of this fetich.

The leading essay, on social solecisms, is the most substantial. It is followed by a collection of *feuilletons* grouped around a central theme and – at their best – carried off with a journalistic vivacity. Her topics include hotel life, tipping, women who smoke, the theatre matinée hat, behaviour in shops and what she called 'the ethics of the motor'.

In her examination of the shibboleths distinguishing the class-structure she begins with forms of speech and moves on to 'certain phrases and expressions which sound the warning note, and caution the unwary lest they should be betrayed into undue familiarity with those not of their caste. . . . Not only is there an exclusive pronuncation' she adds, 'and distinctive expressions, but there are actual possessions which are reserved solely for the use of middle classdom. Napkin-rings, fish-knives, tea-cosies, and oh! I shudder as I write the word, 'tidies' and nightgown cases! (the owner would probably call it a night*dress* case)'.

There are certain details that might catch the eye particularly of a present-day reader accustomed to the expressions 'U' and 'non-U'. One is the reference to 'the terrible habit of putting milk into a teacup before pouring the tea'. Another is the championing of the rights of 'Hons'. It is Agnes and not Nancy Mitford who wrote,

> The decrees of fashion are very arbitrary. It is an unexplained mystery why the courtesy title 'Honourable' is not to be mentioned in polite society, and why it should be excluded from the visiting cards of the honourable possessors of such title.
>
> But to put 'Hon' on one's cards is not the only outrage that can be committed on visiting cards. One card containing the joint names of husband and wife is very shocking to one's sense of decency. A lady I knew carried this reticence to an extreme when she spent her time separating the works of male and female authors on her bookshelves.

It is not without significance that Nancy Mitford was a great-granddaughter of one of Agnes's Stanley aunts – Blanche, Lady Airlie. One may wonder if the 'Hons and Rebels' had read *The Social Fetich*. In any case they shared the traditions that Agnes described as 'an inheritance from the old Whig-School, who joined to their natural, aristocratic instincts the critical faculty developed by intelligence and culture.'

Much of *The Social Fetich* is obviously written tongue-in-cheek. Indeed its merit is that it maintains a serio-comic balance. At times Agnes makes herself the target for her humour – 'I occasionally persuade myself that my health requires a glass of port-wine (which it does not).' In the end she makes it clear that a mystical aristocracy of blue blood is a delusion, since it is open to anyone to learn the fetichistic pass words and practices of contemporary society –

> Not for one minute would I have it supposed that in any of the foregoing remarks a serious attempt is made to cast ridicule or contempt on the *middle* classes; I have endeavoured to point out how superficial the distinction is between the two uppermost classes, which are becoming so merged as to be scarcely distinguishable except by the above superficialities.
>
> Let any one acquire these superficial finishing touches of diction, phraseology, and habits fundamentally and 'by heart', and I defy any one – well, almost anyone – in normal circumstances to detect a flaw.
>
> To believe there is a further difference is a magnificent conceit, a superstition which, alas! clings and is hard to shake off.

The book excited the sort of amused interest one might expect and Agnes was given the role of arbiter in social etiquette. In a letter to Lady Dorothy Neville, Frederic Harrison wrote 'I make heroic efforts to see you whenever I have to be '*in town*' – an expression which Lady Grove says is *vulgar* – is it – you know!' *Punch* lampooned the book in a surprisingly leaden-footed piece by A.A. Milne. *The Daily Chronicle* promptly invited her to contribute articles on similar subjects, and *The Daily Despatch* soon followed with the same request. Hilaire Belloc wanted her to include typewritten letters in the category of socially outrageous things and sent her the following letter (typewritten) to say so –

> Dear Lady Grove,
>
> If you really do want something quite impossible consider the typewritten letter, but it is all one to Almighty God. Your book afforded me immense pleasure, and you cannot complain that the public has not seized it. I do not know who your publisher is, but if he says there is no profit, put him in jail. Do not tell him I said this, as it would be the end of my Career. If I have one. I shall be away on the 26th, but when Parliament meet I will come and see you suddenly and am,
>
> Your obedient servant to command,
> H. Belloc.

At about the same time she engaged Bernard Shaw in a brisk exchange of letters in the columns of *The Academy*. Shaw had apparently made some light-hearted reference to a Satanic interlocutor at one of his lectures. Convinced that this applied to herself, Agnes wrote

> Mr. Bernard Shaw appears to be no happier in his conception of the Devil than he is in his conception of the Deity: for it was I who spoke to him after his lecture, and I saw no one else in the vicinity who came even approximately near to the description he gives of his interlocutor. But I will not pretend that Mr. Shaw is the first person who has made the same mistake.
>
> Mr. Shaw is quite right. His poor mediocre second-rate little god I would not even know, much less worship. . . . Whether you call yourself a mono- or a poly-theist the term *God* has always implied an object of worship or adoration. It must be

humbling, I should have thought (and yet in Mr. Shaw this result is not apparent) to have to make apologies for one's God as one would for a blundering footman or a performing poodle whose deficiencies become too obtrusive; and to have to say 'he means well but his training is inadequate' cannot be conducive to awe or reverence. Mr. Shaw must find a name other than 'God' for his 'brave poor thing' by whose cumulative effort he is content to believe himself to have been created, and leave the conventional appellation to the mysterious and inscrutable Being who, according to my religion, manifests himself to mortals through their noblest achievements and their highest and purest emotions.

To this Shaw made a splendidly characteristic reply, in his most exuberant manner.

Sir,

Lady Grove confesses to being the beautiful-diabolical lady who incarnated the deadly Sin of Pride, and scorned the god who contrived so vulgar a makeshift as this world, and contrived it so clumsily even at that. The confession leaves me nothing to withdraw: the situation remains unaltered. Lady Grove will not worship the god whw made me, because I am a blunderer; because my brain cannot grasp the universe nor my hand trace one perfect line; because even those noblest achievements and highest and purest emotions which she admits to be divine manifestations are hampered in my case with daily necessities of the most undignified and unpresentable kind, and with modes of physical expression so ludicrous that I shrink from penning even this discreet allusion to them.

'I would not even know, much less worship, his poor mediocre little god', she says. Worship him she need not: know him she must, for the facts are the facts. Blake, contemplating the tiger, exclaimed, 'Did He who made the lamb make thee?'; and I have no doubt that he would have said the same had he been comparing me with Lady Grove. But Blake knew that the answer would be Yes; and I flatter myself that Lady Grove and I were fashioned by the same hand – only, as I came first, the hand improved with practice. I will even go so far as to include in the family 'the blundering footman and the performing poodle.'

(By the way, do footmen ever blunder? They seem to me to be the only people who never do – doubtless because their credit and livelihood depend on their infallibility in their own orbit. And why should a performing poodle be apologised for? Apologise, if you will, for those who are so blind to the charm of their friendly natural ways as to teach them silly human tricks; but the only apology which concerns the poodle is the apology due to itself. You see what Lady Grove's theology leads to! – insults to footmen and injustice to poodles. As if there were not generals and bishops and judges to serve as examples of blundering, and amateurs of all the arts to reproach for inept performances!)

I was taught the creed of Lady Grove's theology when I was a little child by an Irish servant. It ran this way:

God made man; and man made money,
God made bees; and bees made honey,
God made Satan; and Satan made sin;
And God made hell to put Satan in.

This disposes of the problem of evil in a very lucid manner, to the satisfaction, apparently, of Irish servants and English ladies; but I have grown out of it, somehow, and find myself inspired to reduce its four whitewashed and blackwashed gods to one classically grey one.

G. Bernard Shaw.

By way of a postscript to the correspondence Bertrand Russell wrote to Agnes, 'You and Shaw both believe too much for me: I think the word 'God' in all the senses I have ever seen assigned to it, represents a fiction. But I particularly dislike Shaw's view that the creation of himself shows that God is coming on'.

In 1908, the year following the publication of *The Social Fetich*, Agnes brought out another new book. This was *The Human Woman* in which she 'does not deal with the arguments in favour of extending the franchise to women (since they are the same as for men) but with the variety of arguments put forward *against* doing so'. Her nine chapters incorporate articles which had appeared in *The Nineteenth Century and After*, *The Fortnightly Review*, *The Cornhill* etc., and display a real sharpness of intellect and a considerable background of relevant reading. Her own practical experience on her local Board of Guardians is brought to bear appropriately in the chapter entitled 'On Women in Assemblies': she is particularly good on women's voluntary work in local government.

Her opponents, actual and imaginary, tend to offer lightweight targets which are easily hit. Her tendency to diffuse her energy in digressions is a congenital failing, and occasional formalisms and stiff phrases are apt to cramp her natural vivacity – mainly when she strives too hard to be magisterial. With those reservations it must, however, be said that *The Human Woman* is her most substantial work – animated, vigorous, sincerely felt, at times humorous and always aggressive in debate. She had been an early and staunch campaigner, but she was no militant. Perhaps it was her historical sense, as a child of the Whig aristocracy, which persuaded her that the gradual extension of the suffrage which had proceeded by stages in the course of the nineteenth century would shortly reach her personal goal, by the force of reasoned argument, in the twentieth. In her view the militants were inculcating 'the false idea of the antagonism of sex', but she had the generosity to add 'However mistaken some of us may think their methods, let us at least give credit for sincerity of motive and singleness of aim.'

Hardy did not see the book before it appeared, though he might have already read and perhaps supervised some of the chapters as separate essays during Agnes's apprentice years. In 1908, when Agnes was preparing the book, Hardy and Emma did not move into London for the season and consequently Agnes lost the customary opportunity for easy exchanges of visits. In a letter during August Hardy explained that, for essential business in London, he had had to 'flit up and down to an hotel': he had heard nothing about her forthcoming book, but it sounded promising.

When she sent him a copy of *The Human Woman*, he acknowledged it as 'a series of brilliant and able essays, which all who favour woman suffrage should be grateful for'. Her tribute to John Stuart Mill as 'the greatest thinker of modern times' would have pleased Hardy. So also, if he noticed it, would the reproduction on the title page of Agnes's bookplate in which were incorporated the names of the books and authors she most admired – among them Tennyson's *Oenone*, Shelley, Petrarch, Tolstoy, Morley's *Life of Gladstone*, Victor Hugo and Thomas Hardy.

What was to be her final book appeared two years later, in 1910. It was a further selection of essays from her ephemeral journalism, collected under the embracing title of 'On Fads'. Its contents date from her earliest acquaintance with Hardy, one of the reprinted essays being 'What Children should be Told'. The extent to which their friendship had matured during the intervening years is reflected in the tone of a letter Hardy wrote to acknowledge her congratulations on his receipt of the Order of Merit. The warmth of his invitation to visit Max Gate is undeniable –

> Why don't you motor over to see us on Monday (Bank Holiday)? It will be impossible for you to go and do anything important, and if you drop in here in the afternoon you will be a godsend. You could come in a hour.
>
> Your affectionate friend
> Thomas Hardy

The publication of *On Fads* drew from Hilaire Belloc an amusing request for a review copy –

> When is your new book to be in my hands? Send it to me and not to the paper and I will do an article on it, then if the 'Morning Post' won't publish it I will get it published elsewhere. Roughly speaking, the Morning Post will never publish anything which can be of any advantage to its readers, or its staff, or its proprietors. It is like the Catholic Church, it survives in spite of its blunders and follies and appears to be lacking in any human guidance. It is perhaps a special department of Journalism run by the Holy Spirit.
>
> I will read your book right through from cover to cover to find out where you speak of me, for I count all books, newspapers and magazines as worthless unless they contain my name.
>
> Don't compare yourself to a puppy and me to a mastiff. In features I more nearly resemble the pug. What kind of fads have you been writing about? Send me the book at once that I may find out. Send it to the Reform Club.
>
> It is a marvel to me that people who are not compelled to write should have to write. You write very well: only every now and then you write whiggishly, which is not criticism of the goodness of the writing but only of the politics. Are you a good Radical? I doubt it!

Reading today the Press reviews of *On Fads* leaves one wondering why she published nothing further. The book was as well received as she could have wished. The critic in *T.P.s Weekly* wrote 'One gets the impression of listening to a brilliant talker who has read everything, been everywhere, and knows everybody'. The *Observer* found in the book 'the lustre of a fine heart'. With three books to her credit in four years one might suppose she was on the crest of the wave.

Belloc's reference to 'people who are not compelled to write' seems to have prompted some kind of misgivings in Agnes. A letter of Hardy's a month later sought to reassure her, stressing that he saw no reason why she should not go on writing provided she liked doing it for its own sake and not for ulterior motives. And he commented shortly afterwards that her book had been '*very* well received by the Press, I think – as it deserved to be'.

Whatever the reason Agnes's career as a minor celebrity of the period seems to have turned towards obscurity after 1910. It was almost as if the death of King Edward marked the end of an epoch for her.

Chapter Seventeen

With no diaries to go on, and very few letters, it is difficult to define Agnes's way of life in the years 1911 to 1914. Probably for financial or health reasons, or some combination of both, she had withdrawn from London to Sedgehill by the beginning of 1910. In April of that year Mary Arnim wrote 'I wish you still lived in London'. In June Hardy referred to an improvement in her health since she gave up living entirely in London. He had thought, and said, that the London atmosphere was harmful to her. Nonetheless she was again ill in April 1911. An anonymous note from a well-wisher – 'one who has read Lady Grove's books' – wished her a speedy recovery.

She must have recovered well enough to involve herself during May in the wedding of her elder daughter, Honor, to a Russian officer, Colonel Nikola Golejewski, who subsequently became Assistant Chief of the Russian Imperial General Staff. Also leaving the family circle in 1911 was Gerald, who joined the British South African Police in Rhodesia. He remained in Africa when war broke out in 1914, serving in German south-west Africa and in the East African campaign. Oenone became a V.A.D. nurse. By 1915 Rushmore had been converted by Alex's wife, Ruth, into a hospital or convalescent home with twenty beds for wounded soldiers, and Oenone was helping there. She could live at home, at Sedgehill, and was a close companion to Agnes at this time. The 1915 diary shows Agnes in pain and apparently taking a pain-killing drug regularly. She also had a Turkish bath installed as part of her therapy.

The writing of this year's diary is low-keyed, monotonous and dispirited. Often the entries have little to say beyond 'very tired, much pain' or 'Had Turkish bath'. Most days she tried to go out for a ride in her motor car or on her bicycle. She saw few people apart from Oenone, 'Fard' (Walter) and the servants. 'Beb' (young Walter) was at boarding-school. She had written immediately to Hardy to congratulate him in 1914 on his second marriage, and the warmth of his reply – with its invitation to motor over to Max Gate for lunch – must have pleased her, but the deepening isolation of the war years weakened the ties of friendship. The London season and the literary tea-parties belonged to a rapidly fading past, obscured by the protracted anxieties and sudden bereavements that accompanied each new list of young men killed, wounded or ominously 'missing'. Walter's cousin Aimée de Hoghton lost her son, Guy; so likewise did Agnes's sister, Alice, when Harold Lubbock died in action with the Grenadier Guards.

Even worse was in store for Walter's sister, Kate. Widowed in 1914 she lost her elder son, Eddy, in 1915, and in the following year her other son, Harry, was reported missing. Walter and Agnes did what they could to comfort her and Agnes was staying with her at Botley on June 20th when, as the diary records –

> Kathleen and I were playing croquet after tea when the letters were brought out. She opened one with OHMS on it and after reading a few lines said in a whisper, 'Oh my God'. I went to her and read that Harry had been found dead near Thiepval – identified by his disc. Poor Kathleen behaved marvellously, so brave and wonderful but it's too heartbreakingly sad.

It is against that sort of background that one may perhaps understand most readily the mounting appeal during the war years of those new systems of faith which appeared to liberate the human spirit from its bondage in the sufferings and carnage of the flesh – spiritualism, for instance, or Christian Science. In the case of Kate Pleydell it was Christian Science that she embraced. This was also the new stage in St. George's highly individual pilgrimage, and Agnes too adopted it for a time. In a letter to Oenone she explained that she was treating Oenone's cold by remote Christian Science technique, and she later applied this telepathic method to help Oenone to give up smoking. It was not long, however, before Agnes became scornful of the 'infallibility' of Mrs. Eddy in the eyes of some of her followers, and she admitted a twinge of apostasy when, in order to please Walter, she took some of the pills prescribed by their doctor for her persistent bowel complaint. Her references to Christian Science end with her reluctant conclusion that its practitioners and their methods cannot cure her 'di'.

While it was the slaughter of the young which dominated all news, public and private, an older generation was quietly slipping away. Aunt Maude, that firm and commanding rock in the whirlpools of Agnes's youth, died in 1915 – an event which might have gone unnoticed at Sedgehill, had not Agnes chanced to see a newspaper report three days later. There seems to have been little communication between them in the previous twenty years and Aunt Maude's will gave no indication of a special relationship. To Oenone Agnes complained that she had been left only £1000, and exclaimed jealously 'All those rich Stanleys, who weren't even her godchildren. . . . and she can't have pretended to think I didn't require the money more than all the others.'

It is a sad comment, and one may indeed wonder if Agnes's need of money had been so evident: certainly not in those bright extravagant Edwardian years when she held her soirées and dinner parties at Bedford Square and revelled in her success as hostess, authoress and social figure. True, Ferne had gone and the Grove estates had gone, but she still had the resources and the style to command the respect of some and to dazzle others.

By 1917, however, there was no disguising her loneliness and general distress. She had no one with whom she could make any conversation worth having. Visitors to Sedgehill were increasingly rare. Oenone was now nursing in London, Gerald was in Africa, Honor in Russia. Beb was beginning to cause anxiety by his childishness and she wondered if he might be mentally deficient. 'I love that little boy', she wrote, 'in spite of the disappointment he is to me!' She had to admit that he was 'very *very* young'. She was beginning to feel like a prisoner at Sedgehill. To get away, to go to London or anywhere else, cost money and she was heavily overdrawn at the bank. She sold her motorcar. With a momentary flash of dry humour she remarked, '*Incidents* are not frequent here'.

In her frustration she poured out her feelings in a stream of letters to Oenone, whose duties as a nurse took her for a time to St. Thomas's Hospital: the fact that this younger daughter was in London gave Agnes a revived sense of contact, at one remove, with the world from which she was virtually exiled. She promised Oenone she would write to 'W.P. and anyone else I can think of to give you a "night out"!' W.P. was of course Willy Peel. In a further letter Agnes was continuing to arrange for Lord Peel and Ella (Lady Peel) to take an interest in Oenone. Then there was Lady Russell. 'Has "Elizabeth" Russell written to you?' Agnes enquired, 'I told her to'. Most important of all was Mary Jeune who, since her husband's elevation to the peerage, was now Lady St. Helier; 'the one person you ought to have been to see in London is Mary, Lady St. Helier, your "Aunt Mary". She is the best Registry office in London for marriage or jobs or anything.' To get Oenone to a dance at Lady St. Helier's became an important task for Agnes, convinced as she was of the value of such opportunities: 'you are sure to meet eligible young men at *some* of these places'.

Oenone's response was as sweet and affectionate as it was ingenuous. To her brother Gerald she wrote, 'I always loved Mummy above everything but she was just the most wonderful Mother that ever was, now she is that and also the most wonderful friend.' However, Oenone was not a suitable vehicle for Agnes's aristocratic ambitions. The young man she found was the impecunious son of her London landlady and not at all eligible. The reverberation in Agnes's diary was correspondingly seismic – 'Oenone came back from London and told me that Billy Matthews had proposed to her and that she was actually thinking it possible to accept him. Stupendous blow. Incredible'.

After ten days of daily letters from Billy he appeared at Sedgehill for a family conference and must have calmed some of Agnes's misgivings. The real stumbling-block was money; Billy did not have the sort of income on which married life was considered to be possible. His mother came at one stage to a willingness to provide £200 a year, but seems to have wavered and fluctuated in recurring bouts of indecision. Contrariwise, Agnes came to favour the match – if only for want of a better one. In one of her letters to Oenone she wrote –

> I daresay you are feeling that if you had gone to Devonport you cd. have fixed up Mrs. Matthews permanently. But my darling I do not believe your future is dependent on the caprice of one old woman. I think that accounts for her not writing to you – she was feeling all wrong and antipathetic to the existing arrangements & *wanting* to upset them. Evidently Billy has very little influence with them. It's no use saying money is a curse – you were prepared to face life with what there was and so was

> he. Then why can't they leave him alone instead of chopping and changing. Of course having written to our lawyer to say that she would give the £200 a year she could be held to it. But of course one doesn't want that sort of thing. I am sorry for poor Billy . . . I doubt if even Billy realises what he would lose if he lost you for good.

But lose her he did. Agnes resumed her conventional methods of propelling Oenone towards a suitable mate, but to no avail: she remained unmarried. Not for her the spectacularly fashionable wedding that her elder sister Honor had enjoyed – 'all those Russian Grand Dukes,' as one of Agnes's friends remarked at the time. As if to point the difference wrought in the six years between 1911 and 1917 the news from Russia became increasingly ominous, and Oenone may have counted herself fortunate that it was not she but Honor who sailed to Petrograd in the autumn of 1916 as the wife of General Golejewski. During the summer of 1917 Agnes was increasingly alarmed by the lack of letters from Honor. Shortly before Christmas she heard that the family was in Odessa, where there had been an outbreak of typhoid. One of Honor's two children, Kira, had died of the disease. Honor herself had been stricken with it on the day of Kira's funeral.

Odessa was not a good place for a Czarist general in such circumstances. 'Koka', as he was known to the family, telegraphed to Agnes for help. Still overdrawn at the bank she had no money to send. She appealed to her sister, Alice Lubbock, who at once provided £100. When there were difficulties over the transmission of the money to Russia Agnes turned to Claud Russell to find some way of communicating with Honor through diplomatic channels. By February 1918 the situation in Russia was worsening. A telegram from Honor appealed for help in getting permits to leave Russia. Balfour, who was then Foreign Secretary, instructed the British consul at Odessa to help General Golejewski and family to proceed to England, but his action was too late: the consul had been compelled to abandon his post and was no longer able to assist.

The manner of Honor's escape with her family from Russia is not described in Agnes's diary which, throughout this period, contains little information of any kind. What is certain is that in the spring of 1919 Honor, Koka and their surviving daughter, Sonia, were at Sedgehill. Agnes meanwhile had been reunited with another of her children, Gerald, who returned from his service in Africa in the summer of 1918. He found his mother obsessively engaged in making vast quantities of jam and anxiously recording the equally vast quantities of coal and coke absorbed by the antiquated cooking and heating system at Sedgehill. These two preoccupations tended to become the major themes in her diary-entries.

Rejoice as she might at news of the Armistice Agnes knew that, in her terms, the peacetime Britain which emerged from the Great War could have little in common with the Britain that preceded it. She no longer had the resources to make any sustained attempt to revive past glories. Her health was poor, her finances even poorer. There were no further Grove assets for Walter to sell, no surplus monies for him to muddle away. The one remaining move for Agnes to make was to sell her diamonds. For her it must have been a capitulation. The precious gems that had added their sophistication to the splendour of her natural beauty were entrusted to Gerald for disposal in London. The money they raised helped to keep her creditors at bay, and to pay the servants' wages.

From necessity her mind ran on methods of economising. She bought some tweed cloth and had it made up locally into a suit for Walter so that he did at least have one presentable outfit for Petty Sessions, where he still sat as a magistrate, and for the shooting-parties to which he was invited. Sonia, his grand-daughter, remembers him as quite indifferent to his appearance and liable to sit on the Bench in any odd assortment of garments. The general impression he left on those who knew him was of a gentle, kindly, ineffectual man, with no head for business or financial matters. 'A poor moth-eaten man' was the phrase used by one of his less charitable contemporaries, 'Agnes had swallowed him up'.

Perhaps she had, but his passivity and her dynamism had been recognised by them both at the outset. In bursts of impatient anger she could strike him, and at other times describe him as 'too sweet for words – so patient and loving.' The bond between them was an enduring one and Walter seems to have relished the pepperiness of his 'dear little pepperpot'.

Where he might have been effective was in the matter of transport, but his relationship with the internal combustion engine was not a happy one. Presumably as a measure of economy he replaced his car with a motorbike and sidecar at about the time of his seventieth birthday, taking Agnes on shopping expeditions to Shaftesbury and Tisbury when this unusual *équipage* could be persuaded to function. It was far from reliable, as her diary indicates. A few days before Christmas, 1922, Walter set off to fetch Sonia from Warminster, returning 'exhausted by struggle with motor b.' How galling it must then have been when Alex's wife, Ruth, 'sent the Rolls Royce with a letter asking us to go to Rushmore for Christmas.' Agnes declined, and for her, Christmas Day was contained in the words 'mended pyjamas, knitted Fard's stockings and read. Damp and dark'.

By this date all her children were abroad. Honor was in Paris; Oenone had just sailed to Egypt, to spend two years at the YWCA in Cairo; Beb had gone to join his uncle Tom in California; and Gerald had turned up in San Diego. The convergence of her two sons on the west coast of America was to some extent a consequence of events in England which must have added to Agnes's heart-ache.

Her earlier misgivings about Beb's childishness took on a more alarmed character when he left school. He spent some time with his aunt Kate – Kathleen Pleydell – and her son-in-law, Mr. Railstone, probably with the intention that he should learn something about farming. Sadly Agnes recorded 'Letters from Railstone and Kathleen saying Beb was "hopeless".' He next went to Hatch House, near Sedgehill, where he began to learn to drive a tractor. An ominous further reference describes Agnes at a garden party where she 'met Canon Abbott and talked to him about Beb's temperance'. He was then eighteen. Three months later he was bound for San Pedro, with the inescapable inference that uncle Tom was being called on as a last resort to 'do something' with the lad. The outcome was striking: within four years Beb married a local Californian girl, and uncle Tom married her widowed mother three years later. Beb's descendants – the last of the Groves of Ferne – were absorbed into the obscurity of American life.

Gerald's departure from England was not so patently inglorious as Beb's but it did follow somewhat abruptly an undefended divorce case in which he was cited as co-respondent and subsequently refused to marry the respondent, after she had sent him a telegram saying plainly 'Mother adamant regarding engagement and subsequent marriage of corespondent and respondent thinks it most important you should come at once to London love from Hermione'. Gerald's reply, as he described it in a letter to Oenone, urged Hermione to recognise that 'the great thing was to keep things quiet' as he was 'much too broke to keep running up to London'; she must 'disillusion her mother if she thought I was heir to a rich baronet with many broad acres'; and she herself 'could marry any day somebody with money enough to keep her in comfort.' He further told her that he had got the opportunity of a pleasant job and 'she must not upset the apple-cart'. There being nothing more to say, he explained to Oenone, 'I ended up in a friendly cheery way'.

The pleasant job that was then in prospect was in Australia, as the private secretary to the governor of the state of Victoria. When Gerald sailed for Melbourne Sedgehill came under a bombardment of telegrams and letters from Hermione. The first, addressed to Gerald, was 'returned to sender, addressee being away'. The next was trained on Walter and was soon followed by a threat that Hermione would follow Gerald to Australia. Agnes entered the fray with a letter intended to overawe 'the woman A' as she referred to Hermione but this only drew the heavier artillery of Hermione's mother, who turned out to be the sister of a duke. 'Very upsetting' was Agnes's comment. For Hermione there was to be no consolation. Her marriage was over, after seventeen years, and one year later she was dead.

Gerald's stay in Australia could hardly have been briefer. After landing in San Diego he found work in Hollywood, at first as an actor but soon as an adviser on the manners and customs of the British aristocracy. In any thesis on the importance of the English butler in American film-making between the wars there must be a footnote on the son of the authoress of *The Social Fetich*.

By 1924 Agnes was feeling herself to be almost a captive at Sedgehill. The motorbike and sidecar had gone, to be replaced by a car – of sorts. 'A good old Ford would have been the thing to have,' she commented ruefully, but Walter bought an Albert, and it almost goes without saying that the makers of the Albert promptly went into liquidation. Spares were unobtainable and the car was therefore unsaleable. The local mechanic did what he could, but the diagnosis was gloomy. 'The fact is', Agnes wrote, 'Fard is *not* good for machinery. The man said the whole engine was "worn" for lack of oil. But Fard *saturates* it with oil, but doesn't simply understand it.'

To Oenone she complained of her frustration and boredom. 'Going nowhere, seeing no-one. We can't go to Ruth's party as there is no sign of the motor nor likely to be'. During the year she had spent only nineteen days in London, mainly for dentistry: 'I did not enjoy any of my trips, it was save and scrape the whole time.' Yet there were moments when she could recapture something of the old glamour. The Larmer Tree fêtes were resumed, with the up-to-date addition of a motor gymkana, and each year there was an invitation to a garden party at Buckingham Palace. Did Claud Russell have some influence in the matter perhaps, or Willy Peel? However it came about, she went to the Palace most years, taking Oenone with her, chatting with Lord Cromer about Thomas Hardy – as she told Hardy when she sent him her annual letter of greetings on his birthday.

Inevitably her letters to Hardy chronicle the passsing of mutual friends – Dorothy Allhusen's husband, Henry, and Florence Henniker. 'I know you will have been sad at Flo Henniker's death', she wrote. 'In her brother's letter to me he said except for her friends she had "nothing to keep her in this dreary world" – what more can anyone have?'

Just how dreary life had become for Agnes was revealed in 1925 when Walter's aged aunt Emma died, leaving him £500. It was the last windfall, the last of the family legacies. Agnes had hoped for £3000, Walter had expected nothing. In a revealing letter to Oenone Agnes explained that the money 'will *just about* and only just clear our local debts, the butcher and the coal man both owed several hundred. But that will be a weight off my mind as we were paying through the nose for the long credit . . . I don't think you have any idea of the nightmare this has been to me, the sense of humiliation and the horror of local debt. I was and always have been powerless to prevent it as nearly all my own money is in Fard's hands and though God knows he doesn't spend much on himself he seems to muddle it all away with never anything to show for it, . . . I had so hoped that Emma's legacy would have cleared the debt at the bank and released a little more income but *that* hope is over.'

It was a sad moment, in the finality of its resignation, for one to whom it had seemed natural to command whatever she pleased. Some who had sat at her table recalled how, in earlier days, she would send back to the kitchen anything that was not cooked to her satisfaction – and her guests might sit for hours in hungry anticipation while a fresh meal was prepared. Some would speak of her vanity, her belief that any of her children could be regarded as 'God's perfect creation'. She herself recognised at last the arrogance with which she had dismissed middle classdom: to Oenone in one of her last letters she wrote 'I expect the nice middle class people in the hotel are just what you thoroughly enjoy and feel at home amongst . . . I can't help thinking how much happier I would have made your life if I had been able to "make friends" at Adelboden, Alassio etc. with all the nice hotel people. I am afraid it simply never entered my head. But I see now that it ought to have!'

Her way was different, a lustrous and vivid passage, comet-like, at once dazzling and precarious. No-one denied her beauty, the fascination of her presence. As a woman and an aristocrat she was perhaps committed, in her generation, to a dilettantism that could not concentrate her talents sufficiently. Hardy, with his exceptional susceptibility to the latent powers in women, responded to the wayward streak of originality in her, the panache, the restless striving. And when she died, in 1926, he created for her an enduring memorial –

I am stopped from hoping what I have hoped before –
    Yes, many a time! –
To dance with that fair woman yet once more
    As in the prime
Of August, when the wide-faced moon looked through
The boughs at the faery lamps of the Larmer Avenue.

I could not, though I should wish, have over again
    That old romance,
And sit apart in the shade as we sat then
    After the dance
The while I held her hand, and, to the booms
Of contrabassos, feet still pulsed from the distant rooms.

I could not. And you do not ask me why.
    Hence you infer
That what may chance to the fairest under the sky
    Has chanced to her.
Yes. She lies white, straight, features marble-keen,
Unapproachable, mute, in a nook I have never seen.

There she may rest like some vague goddess, shaped
    As out of snow;
Say Aphrodite sleeping; or bedraped
    Like Kalupso;
Or Amphitrite stretched on the Mid-sea swell,
Or one of the Nine grown stiff from thought. I cannot tell!

Select Bibliography

General Pitt-Rivers: M.W. Thompson (Moonraker Press).
The Ladies of Alderley: ed. Nancy Mitford (Hamish Hamilton).
The Stanleys of Alderley: ed. Nancy Mitford (Hamish Hamilton).
Autobiography: Bertrand Russell (Allen & Unwin).
The Life of Thomas Hardy: Florence Hardy (Macmillan).
The Collected Letters of Thomas Hardy: ed. R.L. Purdy & M. Millgate (Oxford U.P.).

An account of Sir Thomas Grove's political career appeared in *The Hatcher Review*, Vol. II. 11, Spring 1981 (Salisbury). The historical association of the Pitt family with Rushmore and the genealogical background to the inheritance of General Pitt-Rivers are presented more fully in my *Cranborne Chase* (Gollancz 1980).

Books by Agnes Grove

Seventy-One Days' Camping in Morocco (Longmans Green, 1902).
The Social Fetich (Smith, Elder (later John Murray), 1907).
The Human Woman (Smith, Elder, 1908).
On Fads (Chapman & Hall, 1910).

Photograph Acknowledgements

The permission of Anthony Pitt-Rivers is gratefully acknowledged for the reproduction of the portrait of General Pitt-Rivers by Fred Beaumont. Photographs of this and of the Larmer Tree Gardens in the 1890s have been supplied by the Salisbury and South Wiltshire Museum. The photograph of the Gardens today has been provided by Anthony Kersting, whose photograph of Winkelbury Hill is featured on the book jacket.

Index